Simple Joy

WOMEN · MINISTRY · FRIENDS

Marlene Morrison Pedigo
Linda B. Selleck, Editor

*For my family and friends who walked this journey of
ministry with me, you are God's blessings to me —
For current women in ministry,
in the hope they may be encouraged —
For the next generation of women, may the legacy of faithful
women in ministry to Christ Jesus flourish*

— MARLENE MORRISON PEDIGO

*When all my hopes in them and in all men were gone,
So that I had nothing outwardly to help me,
nor could I tell what to do,
Then, oh then, I heard a voice which said,
'There is one, even Christ Jesus,
that can speak to thy condition;'
And when I heard it, my heart did leap for joy . . .
. . . A great work of the Lord fell upon me,
to the admiration of many,
Who thought I had been dead, and many came
to see me for about fourteen days.
I was very much altered in countenance and person,
as if my body had been new molded or changed.
My sorrows and troubles began to wear off,
and tears of joy dropped from me,
So that I could have wept night and day
with tears of joy to the Lord . . .*

— GEORGE FOX (1624-1691)
founder, Religious Society of Friends (Friends Church)

Unless otherwise indicated all scriptural quotations are from the
New Revised Standard Version of the Bible.

Copyright 2024 Friends United Press

All rights reserved. No portion of this book may be reproduced, stored in electronic retrieval system or transmitted in any form or by means—electronic, mechanical, photocopy, recording or other—except for brief quotations in printed reviews, without the permission of the publisher.

Cover: *Quaker Woman Preaching to Dutch Settlers in the Streets of New Amsterdam*, 1657, anonymous wood carving.

Book design by David Botwinik

Library of Congress Cataloging-in-Publication Data

Names: Pedigo, Marlene Morrison, 1952- author. | Selleck, Linda, editor.
Title: Simple joy : women, ministry, friends / Marlene Morrison Pedigo ; Linda B. Selleck, editor.
Description: Richmond, IN : Friends United Press, [2024] | Includes bibliographical references. | Summary: "Author Marlene Pedigo considers faithful women ministers, from the Bible through the history of Friends (Quakers) to her own experience. She considers the tasks of ministry, and provides examples of times when women fulfilling these tasks have improved the lives of others, have strengthened the church, and have increased the strength and faithfulness of the Friends church"-- Provided by publisher.
Identifiers: LCCN 2024057668 (print) | LCCN 2024057669 (ebook) | ISBN 9780913408285 (trade paperback) | ISBN 9781956149289 (ebook)
Subjects: LCSH: Chicago Fellowship of Friends. | Society of Friends--Clergy. | Society of Friends--Illinois--Chicago. | Quakers--Illinois--Chicago. | Women clergy--Illinois--Chicago.
Classification: LCC BX7649.C53 P44 2024 (print) | LCC BX7649.C53 (ebook) | DDC 289.6092/52--dc23/eng/20250110
LC record available at https://lccn.loc.gov/2024057668
LC ebook record available at https://lccn.loc.gov/2024057669

Friends United Press
101 Quaker Hill Drive
Richmond, IN 47374
friendsunitedmeeting.org

ISBN 978-0-913408-28-5

CONTENTS

FOREWORD ix

CHAPTER ONE *Listening Prayer and Obedience* 1
Mary, Listening to God
    Listening to God 1
    Experiencing Christ Jesus 2
    Challenge of Seeking and Listening for God Today 5
    Listening to God's Call 6

CHAPTER TWO *Discernment* 9
Anna, Sanctuary in the Soul
    Sanctuary in the Soul 9
    Discernment in the New Testament Church 11
    Margaret Fell 12
    Discernment of a Call to Ministry 15

CHAPTER THREE *Evangelism* 17
Samaritan Woman and Christ's Living Water
    What Does It Mean to be Born Again? 17
    Living Water — Worship in Spirit and Truth 18
    A Convinced, Transformed Life 20
    Early Chicago Ministry 25

CHAPTER FOUR *Peacemaker* 27
Canaanite Mother, Prayer, and Peacemaking
    Prayer and Peacemaking 27
    Peacemaking of Early Friends — Mary Dyer 30
    Arrow and Breath Prayers — First Steps of Peace 35

CHAPTER FIVE *Faith and Healing* 37
Daughter
    Daughter, Your Faith Has Made You Well 37
    Have You Ever Been Desperate for a Healing? 40
    Elizabeth Hooton and Ann Branson. 40
    Testimonies of Healing. 44

CHAPTER SIX *A Transformed Life Transforms Others* 47
The Anointing Woman
    Simon the Pharisee and the Anointing Woman 47
    Elizabeth Fry, "The Angel of Prisons" 49
    Elizabeth (Rous) Comstock 53
    Transformational Ministry. 55

CHAPTER SEVEN *Deacon, Minister, Apostle* 58
Mary Magdalene and the Ministering Women
    Mary Magdalene and the Ministering Women 58
    Western Yearly Meeting — Historic Women Ministers. . . . 61
    Embracing an Endangered Testimony 66

CHAPTER EIGHT *Generosity* 69
Mary of Bethany
    Mary of Bethany Listening at the Feet of Christ 70
    Mary of Bethany Confesses Her Need 71
    Mary of Bethany's Generosity. 72
    Ministry of Service 73
    Witness of Service in our Daily Lives 77

CHAPTER NINE *Hospitality and Spirit-Led Worship* 79
Mary, Mother of Mark
    The Birthplace of the Church 80
    Gathered Prayer 81
    The Presence of Christ in the Midst. 84

CHAPTER TEN *Disciple* 88
Tabitha/Dorcas
    Abounding with Deeds of Kindness 88

CONTENTS

    International Friends Women in Ministry 89
    Ministry of Kind Deeds 92

CHAPTER ELEVEN *Prayer and Praise* 95
Lydia and the Women of Philippi
    The Women of Philippi 96
    Bearing the Cross of Christ Jesus 98
    The Power of Praise 101

CHAPTER TWELVE *Church Planter and Elder* 104
Priscilla
    Priscilla and Aquila 104
    Helen and Jefferson Ford 106
    Will the Real Elders Please Stand Up! 109

CHAPTER THIRTEEN *The Body of Christ, the Church* 113
The Romen Women
    The New Testament Church, the Body of Christ 113
    Women in Ministry Among Friends 115
    Letting Our Lives Speak in the Body of Christ 119

EPILOGUE 124

ENDNOTES 126

APPENDIX *Journal and Discuss with Faith in Action* 130
    Chapter One 130
    Chapter Two 131
    Clearness Committee Discernment 133
    Chapter Three 134
    Chapter Four 136
    Chapter Five 138
    Chapter Six 139
    Chapter Seven 141
    Chapter Eight 143

Chapter Nine 144

Chapter Ten 145

Chapter Eleven 147

Chapter Twelve 148

Chapter Thirteen 149

ACKNOWLEDGEMENTS 152

BIBLIOGRAPHY 156

FOREWORD

The inspiration for this book came years ago when I uncovered the stories of the New Testament women compelled to travel in Holy Spirit-led ministry and proclaim the Risen Christ, and learned about Friends women ministers while a student at McCormick Theological Seminary in Chicago. However, if written at that time, the portion of my own ministry pilgrimage within the church would have been short-sighted. It has taken my personal spiritual journey and the seasoning which comes from living in the "School of the Holy Spirit" to write the book you have before you. When I attended a Young Adult Friends Summit Conference and realized there was a hunger to know more about the New Testament women, the legacy of Friends women recorded in public ministry, and how women might minister today, I realized it was time to begin the task. A special thank you goes to the precious Friends who assisted with the creation of this book by giving their testimonies, providing feedback, and editing. You have been one of God's blessings to me in this endeavor!

Each chapter focuses upon the legacy of a New Testament woman in ministry, the witness of a historic Friends woman minister, and my personal experience of ministry in the Friends Church. Throughout is woven an emphasis upon prayer since this book is meant to be savored as a personal devotional, and then shared with a spiritual friend or Sunday School class or study group. Journaling queries, discussion questions, and "Faith in Action" suggestions are provided for each chapter in the Appendix.

Pour a cup of tea. Invite your friends to the table. Then . . .

- Discuss the life of a New Testament women in ministry,

- Learn about the work and travels of historical women in the ministry among Friends,
- Consider the significant blessings and challenges now experienced today by women involved in ministry for Jesus Christ.

It is time to be the change for Jesus Christ, and begin your journey of living prayer through the Holy Spirit!

CHAPTER ONE

Listening Prayer and Obedience
Mary, Listening to God

It was a bitter cold winter night with wicked Chicago rush hour traffic, as I drove home after a hard day at work. My kids were in the back seats as I debriefed out loud about how I was running late due to the circumstances of the day. Essentially, I was complaining and feeling sorry for myself.

Suddenly my six-year-old son spoke truth to my heart. "Mom, you just need to hug Jesus!" Talk about having a holy moment — I heard God speak to me through the voice of a child!

Today it is easy to feel that God is a "million miles" away. How do we listen for God and "hug Jesus" when our lives become difficult and demanding, and when our thoughts and emotions are overwhelming?

Listening to God

God is not silent nor distant. We are all created in God's image to walk in communion with the Lord (Genesis 1-3). Yet we were designed with free will, not with blind allegiance. Our sinful natures break this holy bond (Romans 1-3). It is no surprise that God's message of love sent to restore our relationship is evidenced in the birth of Jesus Christ into a human family.

A young woman named Mary knew how to listen to God. When an angel appeared, Mary was told she would become the mother of Jesus who would "save His people from their sins" (Matthew 1:21). Mary might have felt the request was an impossible task for a recently engaged Jewish girl. Pregnancy outside of marriage could ruin her engagement to Joseph, scandalize her young life, and possibly even lead to death by stoning. No doubt these scenarios flashed through

The Annunciation, by Henry Ossawa Tanner (1859-1937).

her mind bringing a rush of fear. Yet the angel's message was clear and compelling, "Nothing is impossible with God!" Mary's response was willing obedience.

The simplicity of Mary's listening heart is timeless for believers today. Precious revelations, or epiphanies, are not controlled by human will or magical manipulation. Mary listened for God's leading, obeyed God's word, and pondered it in her heart.

Experiencing Christ Jesus

A young man who listened to God was George Fox. As seventeenth-century England struggled with religious reformation and the political turmoil of a civil war, George personally experienced a divine revelation from Christ Jesus which changed his life.

Although George believed in God and came from a religious family, he sought an alternative to the violent and political struggles he witnessed in the state church. George's mother, Mary Lago, came from the stock of English martyrs, most likely George's great-uncle

CHAPTER ONE: LISTENING PRAYER AND OBEDIENCE

Robert Glover.[1] Glover was burned at the stake by the Catholic Church for the right to read the Bible in English. George began to seek a deeper spiritual experience to the alarming conditions he observed around him.

The well-intentioned advice George received from the people in his life is not uncommon for young people to hear today: get a job, get married, join the military, smoke tobacco, or sing Psalms. George found these suggestions did not speak to his condition, and by age twenty spent his free time praying, fasting, and walking in solitude. ". . . I would go into the orchard or the fields, with my Bible by myself."[2] George began to seek the Lord and to listen. One day when all his hope in men was gone and George had nothing outwardly to help him, he heard a voice which said,

> "There is one, even Christ Jesus, that can speak to thy condition;" and when I heard it, my heart did leap for joy.[3]

People from all around the area came to witness the transformation of the Holy Spirit in the life of George Fox and called him a young man with a "discerning spirit."

> My sorrows and troubles began to wear off, and tears of joy dropped from me, so that I could have wept night and day with tears of joy to the Lord, in humility and brokenness of heart.
> Now I was come up in spirit through the flaming sword, into the paradise of God. All things were new; and all creation gave unto me another smell than before, beyond what words can utter. I knew nothing but pureness, and innocency, and righteousness; being renewed into the image of God by Christ Jesus, to the state of Adam, which he was in before he fell.[4]

This direct revelation of the living Christ Jesus and the subsequent transformation of the Holy Spirit led George to gather seekers of Truth into the Religious Society of Friends (Friends Church). Unlike other reformation movements, this was not a movement of clergy breaking away from the established church, often from privileged families. It was an organic lay movement with many young leaders, both men and women, called into ministry. Twelve members of the first group of Friends ministers called the "Valiant Sixty"

Quaker Woman Preaching to Dutch Settlers in the Streets of New Amsterdam, 1657. Anonymous Wood Carving.

were women.[5] George felt being convinced as a Friend led to the restoration we were created to have with God as evidenced in the Garden of Eden. Man and woman were equal partners, who before the Fall walked in holiness with God. Early Friends believed they were reviving "Primitive Christianity."

CHAPTER ONE: LISTENING PRAYER AND OBEDIENCE

I have rejoiced in my faith tradition, the Religious Society of Friends (Friends Church), which has historically "recorded" men and women in ministry since the early generations of Friends in England. We observe an individual's (male or female) mature Christian spirit as Friends, then discern their faithful obedience to a divine call leading to ministry. Then we "record" in our business meetings their ordination of God through the power of the Holy Spirit. This is the cherished tradition of Friends. Today the Lord continues to call into ministry those faithful men and women who are listening and seeking God's will for their own lives.

Challenge of Seeking and Listening for God Today

In this "tyranny of the urgent" world in which we live, it is easy to become controlled by competing external voices, rather than developing our personal relationship with Christ Jesus, and learning to discern the voice of God. A quiet spot for the study of God's word in daily devotions and listening prayer throughout the day is vital if we hope to silence ourselves and to better hear God's voice speak to us. To let our lives speak in ministry, we must faithfully live what we profess — we must "walk our talk." Listening prayer is essential.

John Punshon wrote about the Friends' practice of silent listening prayer in his book *Encounter with Silence*.

> My first steps in the silence were taken in prayer. That was something I already knew how to do. The simple acts of self-examination, confession, thanksgiving, praise, intercession and petition allowed me to give some sort of shape to what I was doing, and thereby increased my confidence. . . .
>
> There is a quality about the silent meeting which goes beyond personal devotions. Our relationship with God stretches two ways. We come into the sanctuary alone, needing to make our peace, but the conditions on which we do so derive from something wider than our own personal needs. We are not islands of consciousness, fragments of understanding, solo voices of praise, pieces of moral rectitude. Within the sanctuary we join with others. We become a people. We hear together. We minister to each other's needs on behalf of the One we have come to worship.[6]

The first step of my call into ministry was learning how to listen to God and to obey.

Listening to God's Call

When I first started to listen for the voice of God, I was inspired by a recorded Friends minister, Dorothy Sinton. Dorothy and her husband John were recorded Friends ministers traveling in the ministry from Ireland Yearly Meeting of Friends. One evening she visited my home church in Iowa and her message was about the importance of placing our lives into the hands of God to be molded and used according to His will (Isaiah 29:13-16). As her profound words stirred and deepened my own faith, I openly committed myself to serving the Lord Jesus Christ to the best of my ability.

As I considered this Divine call to Christ-led ministry, the Lord placed another Friends woman minister into my life, Irma Morris (1916-2009). Irma was the director of a childcare facility at the United Methodist Church in Wilmore, Kentucky, and had been recorded as a Friends minister by Iowa Yearly Meeting. While my husband Steve attended Asbury Theological Seminary, I worked for Irma in the afternoons with school-aged children.

One Saturday afternoon, Irma invited me over to her house to help make homemade noodles which she intended to carry to the Friends fellowship dinner the next day. As we talked together, I learned about her life. She told me it was my great-grandfather, JT Molloy from Iowa, who had recognized her call to public ministry. When she was eighty-seven years old, Irma wrote me a letter describing this moment in her life and her subsequent ministry as a woman:

> In fact, I have discovered some interesting things in my memory bank. I would never have chosen the public life, but a man named Jim Molloy walked from the east side of the church to the west side where I stood one Sunday morning, stuck his old crooked forefinger under my nose and said, 'I am going to live to see the day when you will stand behind that pulpit and preach the Gospel.' No one was more shocked than I. Being a teenager who had been

CHAPTER ONE: LISTENING PRAYER AND OBEDIENCE

raised to be polite, I did not laugh. Although I felt shock and felt it was something to laugh at, I have never forgotten that morning. It is as real as it ever was.

I marveled how my life had intersected with her life while we were living in Wilmore, Kentucky.

As I got to know Irma better, I shared with her my leading to ministry which I had felt while a student at William Penn University. One summer during college, I had attended Explo '72 with other young adults from Iowa Yearly Meeting and heard Billy Graham challenge us to learn how to come down from living on mountaintop experiences to living our faith in the valleys of life in the world. Explo '72 was a Campus Crusade for Christ conference which drew more than 80,000 college and high school students to the Cotton Bowl Stadium in Dallas, Texas. One night as we passed around the candlelight to those next to us in the Cotton Bowl, I heard God's call to ministry for my life.

Irma and I realized there were those in the church who resisted women in ministry leadership. However, the ministry of women who responded to Jesus Christ faithfully can be found in the New Testament. Irma talked to me about the Parable of the Talents (Matthew 25:14–30) and how we are each accountable to God for the stewardship of the life and abilities given to us. What will we say to the Lord when we get to heaven and are asked why we did not use our talents? Don't we want to hear from God, "Well done, good and faithful servant?" Is it acceptable to do nothing because we listen to discouraging voices who say women should not be found in ministry? Talking with Irma, I decided not to be afraid of following my calling and listening with sacred discernment to the voice of God.

A few months later Steve shared with me, after a visit to Chicago, that he felt led to move to the city at the end of the week so he could transfer to North Park Theological Seminary. There he would train for urban ministry, and begin to work in the Cabrini-Green Public Housing Development. I had heard national news stories about Cabrini-Green. There were riots in the streets during the 1960s, when police officers had been killed and the National Guard had been called up to bring control. Scenarios of this flashed through

The William Green Homes, Chicago's Cabrini-Green Public Housing.

my mind. Would God be calling us to step out in faith to go to this community when other churches were fleeing the city to the suburbs?

Steve had grown up in Milwaukee and knew the great need for urban ministry. He felt called to begin this training as soon as possible. A friend in Chicago had invited us to help begin a Young Life chapter in Cabrini-Green. Would we be obedient to God's call?

I went to see Irma. She said that if God was calling Steve to this ministry, He would provide. We must listen and go. I am thankful for the Friends ministers who planted the seeds and cultivated my heart to listen to God. So, this sixth-generation family farm girl from Poweshiek County, Iowa, followed the Lord's leading to begin ministry in one of the oldest public housing developments in Chicago. We embarked on what would become nearly thirty years of ministry in Cabrini-Green.

Are you taking the time to listen?

CHAPTER TWO

Discernment
Anna, Sanctuary in the Soul

When I began ministry in Chicago, I learned to talk to God a lot!

One day as I drove our family van to Oak Street in Chicago's Cabrini-Green housing development, I suddenly realized that police cars were flashing their lights in front of our church. With the street blocked by squad cars, I circled around and approached from a different direction, and slipped into a door to the after-school program with my children, avoiding the yellow crime scene tape. There had been a shooting in front of our meetinghouse, and the blood of the teenage girl was still on the sidewalk. Although the City of Chicago eventually came out to clean the blood away, the shooting of another child in Cabrini-Green pierced my heart. How do we discern a way forward when violence crashes into our existence?

Jesus Christ said He would always be with us, "For where two or three are gathered in my name, I am there among them" (Matthew 18:20). When we open the door of our heart to Christ Jesus (Revelations 3:20), and learn to walk in the Holy Spirit, true sanctuary occurs within us. This concept of prayer and discernment is seen in the life of Anna, the prophet.

Sanctuary in the Soul

There are only three verses in Luke's gospel, found in Chapter 2:36-38, which describe the prophet Anna. As a prophet, Anna possessed the ability to discern God's voice and speak to His people. Luke writes that Anna was eighty-four years of age. If Anna was married between 15 and 16, which often was the custom for young Jewish women, and only lived with her husband for seven years, she would

> *There was also a prophet, Anna the daughter of Phanuel, of the tribe of Asher. She was of a great age, having lived with her husband seven years after her marriage, then as a widow to the age of eighty-four. She never left the temple but worshiped there with fasting and prayer night and day. At that moment she came, and began to praise God and to speak about the child to all who were looking for the redemption of Jerusalem.*
>
> — LUKE 2:36-38

have been in her early 20s at the time she became a widow in the year 63 BC.

This is a significant year in the history of Israel, because it is the date of the conquest of Jerusalem by the Roman military leader Pompey the Great. After a three-month siege, Pompey overcame the resistance in Jerusalem and ended a civil war between the Pharisees and Sadducees. The historian Josephus reported 12,000 Jews fell during the conquest of Jerusalem by the Roman soldiers.[1] Perhaps Anna became a widow at a young age because of this battle. Perhaps living in sanctuary within the Temple she "never left" was a result of this trauma.

Under the occupation of Jerusalem by the Roman Empire, Anna found an indwelling sanctuary which was far more than physical residency in the Jerusalem Temple. A spiritually safe haven seeped into her soul. As her interior sacred space grew deeper, more discerning, wise, and knowing, Anna was led to develop her own spiritual disciplines. She "worshiped there with fasting and prayer night and day" (Luke 2:37). She became exquisitely sensitive to the voice of God.

When Joseph and Mary went to the Jerusalem Temple to fulfill the Jewish purification ritual for firstborn males, Anna saw the infant Jesus and began to praise God! She boldly proclaimed to those present who looked for the "redemption of Jerusalem" that this baby, present in their midst, was their long-awaited Savior (Luke 2:38).

Anna's prophecy concerning Jesus marks the beginning of a transition. The ability to hear the word of God would no longer be only the experience of individual Old Testament prophets. Now spiritual discernment, the ability to understand the leading of the Holy Spirit who speaks the Word of God, became a testimony of the New Testament church.

Discernment in the New Testament Church

In the tenth chapter of the Gospel of John, Jesus declared He was the Good Shepherd. His followers, or "sheep," would hear His voice. We experience Christ Jesus as Friend when we abide in Christ and do His will: "You are my friends if you do what I command you. I do not call you servants any longer, because the servant does not know what the master is doing; but I have called you friends, because I have made known to you everything that I have heard from my Father" (John 15:14, 15). When Christ Jesus is known as Friend (theology), it impacts the organizational structure and decision-making of the church (ecclesiology).

In Acts 15, we discover the Holy Spirit is more than a shared experience at Pentecost. The glory of God (Greek, *doxa of Theou*) is now a shared experience of the church in discernment (Greek, *edoxe*). The New Testament Church discerned a decision in agreement with the Holy Spirit: "For it has seemed good to the Holy Spirit and to us to impose on you no further burden than these essentials" (Acts 15:28). Discernment became an experience of the church.

Early Friends theologian Robert Barclay referred to Acts 15 when he described the Friends process of decision making in his book, *Anarchy of the Ranters*. Elements mirrored by the Religious Society of Friends' monthly meetings for making business decisions, "the sense of the meeting," are:

- Gather the Church
- Testimonies of Spirit-Filled Leaders — Peter, Barnabas, and Paul
- Silence

George Fox at Swarthmoor Hall with the Fell Family, etching by Robert Spence (1871-1964). The taller woman is Margaret Fell.

- Unity with Scripture
- State the Sense of the Meeting — James Acting as Clerk
- Circulate a Decision Minute — "For it has seemed good to the Holy Spirit and to us to impose on you no further burden than these essentials" (Acts 15:28).

Discernment of God's will can ignite the church! Decisions which have been discerned through the power of the Holy Spirit bring glory to God! Discernment and subsequent empowerment for ministry can be seen in the life of one of the earliest Friends women in ministry.

Margaret Fell

Eventually known as the "Mother of Quakerism," Margaret Fell (1614-1702) first heard George Fox preach in June, 1652, writing this of the experience:

> [Fox said] "You will say, Christ says this, and the apostles say this, but what can you say? Are you a child of light and have walked in the light? What you speak, is it inwardly from God?"

CHAPTER TWO: DISCERNMENT

Swarthmoor Hall, by George Lehman.

> This opened me so, that it cut me to the heart. Then I saw clearly, we were all wrong. So, I sat me down in my pew again, and cried bitterly. I cried in my spirit to the Lord, "We are all thieves, we are all thieves. We have taken the Scriptures in words, and know nothing of them in ourselves."[2]

The Holy Spirit convicted Margaret's heart and she listened.

After Margaret became a convinced Friend, she opened Swarthmoor Hall, home to Margaret and her husband Judge Thomas Fell and their eight children, as a spiritual center for Friends worship, meetings, activities, and communications. Fell acted as a secretary through her voluminous correspondence, along with the channeling of funds to traveling Friends ministers in England and abroad. After her husband's death in 1658, Margaret continued serving the growing Friends movement and became a Friends minister herself.

When George Fox was arrested during a visit to Swarthmoor Hall in 1659, Margaret felt called to action. At the age of forty-six, she traveled to London to advocate the release of George and to seek religious toleration for other imprisoned Friends who refused to take an Oath of Allegiance to the Crown. *A Declaration of*

Quaker Principles and Practice from Margaret Fell to King Charles and Parliament, published by Margaret in June of 1660, is the first public Friends peace testimony statement used to seek the release of Friends from religious persecution.

In February, 1664, Margaret was arrested for failing to take an oath and for allowing Friends to gather for worship in her home. She defended this action by stating she was blessed with a home and would worship the Lord in it. She was sentenced to imprisonment and the forfeiture of her property.

Perhaps Margaret's most well-known work that continues to have ecclesiastical importance was *Women's Speaking Justified, Proved and Allowed of by the Scriptures*, written in 1666 while Margaret was in prison. Margaret used Scripture to advocate for and embolden women in ministry. She wrote:

> Let this serve to stop that opposing spirit that would limit the power and Spirit of the Lord Jesus, whose Spirit is poured upon all flesh, both sons and daughters, now in His resurrection — since that the Lord God in creation, when He made man in His own image, He made them male and female. . . . In this true church, sons and daughters do prophesy. Women labor in the gospel. But the apostle permits not tattlers, busy-bodies, and such as usurp authority over the man, who would not have Christ to reign nor speak, neither in the male or female. . . . Christ is the head of the church. . . . Here Christ is the head of the male and female who may speak. The church is called a royal priesthood; so, the woman must offer as well as the man.[3]

Margaret believed the Apostle Paul had no problem with holy women who spoke and labored with him in the Church. Indeed, Paul often included the names of women traveling in ministry with him in his epistle greetings and prayers. Margaret's discernment and obedience in ministry were clear.

Margaret married George Fox in 1669, but was imprisoned again for another year for breaking the "Conventicle Acts" which stated religious assemblies outside the auspices of the Church of England could not include more than five people other than the immediate family. Today we often overlook the fact that the religious freedom we cherish was the result of years of persecution and suffering of Friends men and women.

Discernment of a Call to Ministry

One of the amazing openings for ministry in my life occurred when we began the Chicago Fellowship of Friends. After our move, Steve completed his Masters of Divinity from North Park Theological Seminary in 1978, and I began my first steps towards a Masters of Divinity and Doctorate of Ministry at McCormick Theological Seminary. During this time, we worked to begin a Young Life ministry at LaSalle Street Church in Chicago's Cabrini-Green Public Housing Development, and we both were recorded as Friends Ministers of the Gospel through Iowa Yearly Meeting of Friends. As youth aged out of Young Life, we prayed for ways to continue a ministry with them in Cabrini.

We felt led to stop by Friends United Meeting's (FUM) denominational office in Richmond, Indiana, to talk with their staff about our vision for ministry. The morning before we met with the FUM staff, we knelt by our bedside and prayed for the Lord to lead and guide us according to His will. I sensed the presence of the Holy Spirit as we prayed.

While meeting with FUM staff, we shared photo albums of our youth ministry activities, told stories of changed lives, and spoke of the need for ministry outreach in Chicago's Cabrini-Green Public Housing. The staff listened to our vision for ministry. They determined that we would need to meet with FUM Board members in the fall to share with them our concern for ministry, and, if approved, funding would start in January. The doorway to our two decades as FUM field staff in urban ministry was opening!

That fall, FUM Board members came to Chicago to pray with us and discern the Lord's call upon our lives. If you have a concern for discernment of God's will for your life, you may consider the use of a Clearness Committee. Historically, Friends elders would meet with members of the meeting for clearness concerning memberships in the meeting, marriages, or conflicts within the church. The discernment through the clearness process is a valuable tool among Friends, and was most important in coming to a firm understanding of our future bond with Friends United Meeting. We were approved as FUM Field staff and our salary was funded in 1980. This amazing historical decision of discernment for ministry set in motion a twenty-year call for Steve and myself at the Chicago Fellowship of Friends. The way that opened for us in ministry at Cabrini-Green was truly the leading of the Lord, and all that was accomplished gave Him the glory!

What can you say of Christ Jesus?

CHAPTER THREE

Evangelism
Samaritan Woman and Christ's Living Water

Extreme thirst is excruciating — to be refreshed by water is delightful! One of my fondest memories of climbing to the 14,000-foot summit of Mt. Princeton in Colorado with a group of teens from Cabrini-Green was stopping to drink fresh "living water" from a mountain stream as we descended from the glorious summit view. An unexperienced hiker, I was parched with thirst. I knelt by the stream and drank the cold, pure mountain water from my cupped hands. What did I care about filtering? Although the physical exertions required to complete such an extreme climb may have contributed to my thirst, this "living" water was clearly different from the water I had drunk from the hand-pumped well on my family farm back in Iowa.

People thirst in their life today! A Christian's simple lifestyle communicates that the externals do not overshadow the internals. The focus is upon the message of how to seek and experience a personal relationship with Christ Jesus — to spiritually drink "living water." It is that simple!

What Does It Mean to be Born Again?

Water is an important topic in the early chapters of the Gospel of John, where we note a transition from Jewish purification rituals of water to the importance of receiving Jesus Christ. To appreciate the Samaritan Woman's encounter with Jesus, a study of His earlier teachings is needed.

In this gospel's first chapter, John the Baptist proclaims of Jesus: "... He on whom you see the Spirit descend and remain is the one who baptizes with the Holy Spirit" (John 1:33b). A distinction is drawn between John the Baptist's repentance baptism, which was also a Jewish ritual for proselytes, and Jesus Christ's baptism of the Holy Spirit.

In the second chapter of the Gospel of John, Jesus' first miracle is revealed — His ability to turn water into wine. The water contained in the stone water jars, used for Jewish rituals of purification, was transformed into a testimony of Jesus' identity. We would now be purified through Christ Jesus.

Jesus again talked about water as he attempted to answer the spiritual inquiries of a man named Nicodemus (John 3). As a member of the Sanhedrin, a Jewish ruling council from Jerusalem, Nicodemus was probably wealthy, educated, and influential. Nicodemus came to Jesus at night seeking answers to spiritual questions. Jesus knew the Jews expected a Messiah who would fulfill Old Testament prophecies: a political king with military might who would deliver them from Roman rule. Jesus proclaimed to Nicodemus that the Kingdom of God was a spiritual birth; it meant to be "born from above." Nicodemus said to Him, "How can anyone be born after having grown old?"

Jesus was speaking of a deeper baptism of the Spirit in one's heart. This was an unexpected, important teaching from Jesus that challenged Nicodemus beyond being physically born into Jewish faith and keeping Jewish traditions. To many Jews, faith was tied to culture. To Jesus, the Kingdom of God was more than religious nationalism — it was for all people. Those who enter the Kingdom of God must have this spiritual birth that Jesus proclaimed. God's gift of love, His Son Jesus Christ, is for the salvation of the world (John 3:16)! This was a new and radical message to a Samaritan woman.

Samaritan Woman, Living Water

One day Jesus and His disciples stopped at Jacob's Well at Shechem, Samaria. Jesus rested at the well while the disciples went into town for food (John 4). When a Samaritan woman came to the well alone at mid-day for water, Jesus asked her for a drink.

It shocked the Samaritan woman that Jesus would speak to her. She knew the Jews considered Samaritans unclean. Jesus gained her attention with His request for water, then revealed He knew she had five husbands. He took the time to talk with her and to offer her "living water" (John 4:10-14).

Jesus' discussion about "living water" and worship occurred at Jacob's well, a significant historic religious site for Abraham's descendants. In Genesis 12:6-8, Abram left his hometown to answer a call from God. When he arrived at this site inhabited by the Canaanites who worshipped the false god Baal, Abram stopped at an oak tree at Shechem to build an altar and worship.

> *Jesus said to her, "Everyone who drinks of this water will be thirsty again, but those who drink of the water that I will give them will never be thirsty. The water that I will give will become in them a spring of water gushing up to eternal life. . . . Let anyone who is thirsty come to me, and let the one who believes in me drink. As the scripture has said, 'Out of the believer's heart shall flow rivers of living water.'"*
>
> — JOHN 4:13-14; 7:37B-38

The Lord appeared to Abram and promised he would be given the land. In Genesis 33:18-20 Jacob, grandson of Abraham, purchased land and built an altar at Shechem. After the Babylonian Exile, the Samaritans built a temple on Mt. Gerizim, near Shechem. At the time of Jesus, they did not feel the need to go to the Jerusalem Temple which had been re-built by the Romans.

Jesus was not going to be drawn into a debate about whose site was the most holy for true worship. The exterior site was not to supersede the preparation of an attitude of worship. Jacob's Well did not represent the fresh "living water" of spiritual worship which Jesus wanted to emphasize. Jesus confronted the traditions of the Samaritans, too. From His discussion of water comes an amazing teaching: "God is spirit, and those who worship Him must worship in spirit and truth" (John 4:24).

In this longest individual dialogue in the gospels, Jesus revealed to the Samaritan woman that He was the Messiah and the Samaritan woman understood (John 4:25, 26). Not only did she accept Jesus as the Christ, but she rushed into the city to tell others, leaving her waterpot behind at the well. Through the Samaritan woman's evangelistic ministry, her neighbors came to believe that Jesus was "truly the Savior of the world" (John 4:42). Evangelism occurred as the "living water" flowed through her!

The "living water" available through Christ Jesus was demonstrated as superior to water rituals when Jesus encountered a lame man who had waited thirty-eight years to be placed in the pool of Bethesda for healing (John 5:1-9). Supplanting the Jerusalem pool's water ritual, Jesus asked, "Do you want to get well?" Ignoring the man's excuses and reluctance, Jesus challenged him, "Stand up, take your mat and walk." The man was immediately healed as he obeyed.

Finally, as the Jewish leaders challenged Jesus, He again announced his identity as the source of the "living water" which would flow through those who believe in Him. "Let anyone who is thirsty come to me, and let the one who believes in me drink. As the scripture has said, 'Out of the believer's heart shall flow rivers of living water" (John 7:37b-38). The Samaritan Woman's spontaneous evangelism was a powerful witness of this reality. As the "living water" of Christ Jesus flows through our lives we too become powerful witnesses — and evangelism occurs!

A Convinced, Transformed Life

This radical nature of worship transformed early Friends who understood the importance of Jesus' emphasis of Holy Spirit baptism (John 1:33), the indwelling of the Holy Spirit. At that time, people were baptized with water at birth into the Church of England. George Fox realized that an outward water ritual was not to be equated with worship in Spirit and Truth. George called those Christians, who professed Christianity without a transformed life, "professors." As he preached, George called people to be convinced of the Truth of Christ Jesus and "show forth a Christian life." He wrote:

> I preached the Truth amongst them, directing them to the Lord Jesus Christ to be their teacher, and to the measure of His Spirit in themselves, by which they might be turned from darkness to

CHAPTER THREE: EVANGELISM

George Fox, by Leopold Grozelier.

light, and from the power of Satan unto God. I warned them all that they should do no violence to any man, but should show forth a Christian life: telling them that He who was to be their Teacher would be their condemner if they were disobedient to Him. . . .

. . . I obeyed the Lord God, went up on the cross, and declared unto them that the day of the Lord was coming upon all their deceitful ways and doing, and deceitful merchandise; that they should put away all cozening and cheating, and keep to Yea and Nay, and speak the truth one to another. So, the Truth and the power of God was set over them.[1]

When we are convinced of the Truth of Christ Jesus and allow the "living water" to flow in our lives, it is a witness to a deep Holy Spirit baptism. Our life changes as God's love is poured into our hearts (Romans 5:1-5). As we walk daily in the Holy Spirit, our lives speak. Incarnational evangelism is a powerful witness of Jesus Christ and what it means to worship in Spirit and Truth.

The concern of Friends to spread their message led traveling ministers to the American colonies. In spite of persecution, often

Quaker Meeting in London: A Female Quaker Preaches from the Balcony, 1723, by Bernard Picard (1673–1733).

a female Friends minister traveled in the ministry with a younger Friends woman. Margaret Hope Bacon writes in *Mothers of Feminism* how frequently Friends women were involved in traveling ministry. "Of the first eighty-seven ministers to visit New England from 1656 to 1700 according to one calculation, twenty-nine, or approximately thirty-three percent were women. This does not include those who traveled with their husbands."[2]

The witness of a transformed faithful life among the early Friends is found in the ministry of Susanna Morris (1682–1755). Born in England to members of the Religious Society of Friends, the Morris family moved to Philadelphia in 1701. Of the five daughters in this family, four of the girls eventually became Friends ministers. In addition to being a wife and mother of thirteen children, Susanna began to travel extensively in Friends ministry beginning at age twenty-nine. Susanna wrote in her journal that if the Lord would give her strength, she would obey the leading to travel in ministry.

CHAPTER THREE: EVANGELISM

> . . . I would not disobey Him but go on His errands wherever, whenever or whatever He was pleased to require . . . a weighty concern of mind for several years (had been) to cross the great ocean in Truth's service where the Lord might be pleased to lead me. But I was so full of the Reasoner that I believe I did displease my God. (I) was so far in debt to Him that He was pleased to put me in prison a long year and I never had in that time to open my mouth by way of testimony. After I had true strength given me to make those promises, my mouth was opened and my tongue was loosened and I was sent over the seas[3]

Disobedience to the call of ministry was a weighty concern among Friends. Instead of obedience to the Lord for ministry, the "Reasoner" was seen to keep women from being faithful. The evangelistic ministry of Susanna Morris helped Truth gain ground in the hearts of people. It was a matter of joy to Susanna's soul.[4]

Discernment of a call to ministry is also seen in the life of Ruth Follows (1718-1809), a recorded Friends minister for sixty years from Leicestershire, England. Her *Journal* records the Lord's dealings in her life when very young and the example of her godly parents. Even when Ruth left her parents' counsel, the Lord was working in her young life through His sharp reproofs.

> (The Lord) stopped me in the midst of my career, and took off my chariot wheels, so that I could not overthrow nor yet keep the pure Seed in bondage; for He was pleased to let me see my state, and very often did He make me to confess my sins before Him, and with tears implore His mercy; and I can truly say, I witnessed Him to be a God hearing prayer. But, oh! Yet was I unwilling to forsake my iniquity, and was for reserving a part, such as I best liked; but the Lord who calls for the whole heart would not accept a half-offering. . . .[5]

She also discerned the Lord's leadings when she felt called to ministry.

> . . . O, what peace did my soul enjoy, when I had given up in pure obedience to the Lord's requirings, which was about the beginning of the twelfth month, 1747, when my mouth was first opened in a public manner at our week day meeting at Castle Donnington, I being about the thirtieth year of my age.

In a little time after, I heard that Elizabeth Fletcher, a Friend in Derbyshire, had a concern on her mind to visit the counties of Huntington, Cambridge, Norfolk, Suffolk and Essex, so to London, in order to visit that great city, and was inquiring where she might meet with a companion who had the same concern.

This took such hold of me when I first heard of it, that it struck like a dart; but I would not have consented to it, if I could have had peace in the refusal; for I let in many reasonings against it, and thought but few like me travelled, and could not see how way was to be made without a great deal of trouble . . . and having just appeared in the ministry, and being a poor weak creature in spiritual things, I could not think what service I could be of to any, except it were to Elizabeth Fletcher, who was a very weakly woman.

But I was made to drop these reasonings, and leave all to the Lord, who can and does make way when we can see no way; so, in obedience to His pure mind and will, I left all to His divine protection, my dear husband and sweet babes, my eldest about six, and youngest about three years old. I thought this a great trial, and it seemed at times to come very near my life; but as I stood resigned to the will of God, He gave me strength in weakness, and His holy arm bore me up through many deep exercises that I met with in this journey.

And blessed be His powerful name! The same arm that took me from my nearest connections in life, also brought me home again in peace; and as I was preserved, so were my dear husband and children; and we both have cause to give all honor and glory to God, who is alone worthy, now and forevermore.[6]

Terry Wallace remarks about these early Friends women actively traveling in Christ's ministry. Editor of the writings of Margaret Fell, Wallace writes, "They were followers, not of male leaders but of their One Guide and Leader, Jesus Christ. In following Him and His direction, they became leaders in their own right, spiritual equals with their male counterparts, and spiritual equals who often carried the gospel message to new cities and countries ahead of those counterparts."[7] They were a significant influence in shaping the direction of the Religious Society of Friends.

The faithfulness to a ministry call continues today. People still seek a living, "life-changing" faith which witnesses to the world around us. Do we have messengers for our generation?

Early Chicago Ministry

Shortly after we arrived in Chicago, my husband Steve developed a sports team with Cabrini teens who wanted to play basketball. One of the Cabrini young men knew of a gym where we could play in another neighborhood. Everyone agreed to go since finding a gym in Chicago's winter weather is a great opportunity — especially when it was free! Little did we know we were soon to have a "teachable ministry moment" about the invisible turf boundary lines of Chicago gangs.

After the basketball game began, verbal banter, or "signifying," occurred between the teams. Before I knew it, the trash talk had escalated to physical shoving. Eventually a fight broke out. Rather than the referees stopping the players from fighting, the conflict erupted as teens in the bleachers rushed onto the basketball court. Now we had a brawl. Gym staff worked to separate the teens and locked our team inside the building as they called the police. I was in a state of shock. We had unknowingly crossed into the turf of a neighborhood gang. When we emerged from the gym, the church van was vandalized with flat tires and broken lights. We called for a ride home.

"How long are you going to stay?" a teen asked. The dream stage of ministry was over!

A local Catholic priest shared with us that in urban ministry, we must nail our personal issues to the cross and seek healing for ourselves before we can effectively minister. Otherwise, our own woundedness is triggered by the pain of others. I needed to nail my fears to the cross — to daily die to self and rise to follow Christ Jesus.

We were called to an incarnational ministry for Christ Jesus. We needed to "earn the right to be heard" to effectively share His life-changing message. The young people we hoped to reach regularly faced the reality of this violence. Would we be willing to step into their world and live out our Christian lives in relationship with them?

A daily baptism was needed to let the "living water" of Christ Jesus flow through our lives to others.

The next few months we continued to build our relationship with the youth on the basketball team. Besides the games, we invited them over to our apartment afterwards for a meal of sloppy joes, spaghetti, pizza, lasagna or pig-in-the-blankets. Afterwards we played Uno or Pit. They started to invite their friends. That summer we took teens to the Young Life Frontier Camp to make the hike up to the 14,000-foot Mt. Princeton summit in Colorado. During our camp sessions we shared about what it meant to make a commitment to Christ Jesus, and gave an invitation to our teens. That fall we began our first Young Life club meeting at the LaSalle Street Church Intern House, which overflowed with one hundred young people present.

Deep baptism of the living water of Jesus Christ was occurring in myself. A thirty-year ministry to the Cabrini-Green community had begun in our lives.

__Have you experienced the deep baptism of Jesus?__

CHAPTER FOUR

Peacemaker
Canaanite Mother, Prayer, and Peacemaking

We acquired an old school building, the St. Philip of Benizi Catholic Church, which was the first Sicilian parish in Chicago built by the Servites of Mary Order of the Catholic Church in 1919. Located at 515 West Oak, this ministry site was between two Cabrini gang turfs. During Prohibition the area had been known as "Death Corner" since approximately fifty homicides had occurred here. Although the residents and the illegal substances changed when the area was transformed into public housing, a legacy of violence continued. What a great location for a historic peace church!

At first the building looked like it had been in a war zone — bullet holes were in the front door, windows were shot out, paint was peeling, the roof was leaking, old drug needles were in the stairwell, and broken glass glistened in the adjacent vacant lot. While some saw a property on the edge of demolition, we saw an opportunity for work crews and ministry. It became an oasis of peace, the Chicago Fellowship of Friends.

Prayer and Peacemaking

The witness for peacemaking is seen in the life of Jesus Christ and those who follow Him. One peacemaking woman who encountered Jesus was the Canaanite mother. To understand this encounter, we need to inquire into the events that occurred before this woman met Jesus.

In Matthew 14, the gospel writer reports the beheading of Jesus' cousin John the Baptist by Herod Antipas, one of the Roman rulers. John had confronted Herod about his marriage to Herod's sister-in-law Herodias, which resulted in John's arrest. As John languished in prison, Herodias' daughter performed an alluring dance for his birthday which prompted Herod to promise her anything she desired. The dancing daughter asked for the head of John the Baptist, which was delivered to her on a platter!

What a wicked, salacious act by Herod, who had considered John a holy man. John the Baptist's disciples sought out Jesus to report John's beheading by the Roman ruler (Matthew 14:12). No doubt they wondered how Jesus would respond to this violent execution of the blameless John. In Luke 13:32 Jesus had called Herod a fox, or an "unclean animal." Would Jesus stand up to this corrupt Jewish ruler in defense of His cousin's death?

When Jesus heard this tragic and devastating news, His first response was an attempt to withdraw to a secluded place by Himself. This was a common practice of prayer found in the life of Christ Jesus. However, the people were not to be dismissed, and when Jesus saw a great crowd gathering, ". . . He had compassion for them and cured their sick" (Matthew 14:14). Mark described the crowd as "sheep without a shepherd" (Mark 6:34).

After Jesus taught them many things, He performed an amazing miracle to communicate His identity and purpose to the immense crowd. The extraordinary and inexplicable feeding of the 5,000 people on the mountainside would remind the Jewish people of the life-giving manna sent from God when the Children of Israel wandered in the wilderness. This comparison to Moses dramatically declared Jesus' true identity as the long-awaited and promised Messiah. It revealed the source of spiritual nourishment available through Christ Jesus. On the eve of Passover, Jesus the Messiah and Prince of Peace did not choose a violent response to revenge the death of His cousin.

However, the opportunity for conflict was not over. The Jerusalem Pharisees and scribes came to confront Jesus about this miracle (Matthew 15). They wondered why He did not keep the tradition of the elders and the ritual of hand washing. Jesus' response to them was to talk about the heart of man. This inner spiritual condition is what truly makes one unclean. A stark difference is drawn between Jesus' miracle to feed 5,000 people, and the Jerusalem religious leaders' response about keeping the ritual of hand washing on the mountainside! Again, we see that for Jesus it was not about the exterior water observance.

In the following passage in Matthew, He will minister to an "unclean" woman. Jesus and His disciples traveled along the Mediterranean coast to Tyre and Sidon, two important cities of ancient Phoenicia which had a strong Greek Hellenistic culture. Here Jesus encountered a woman who would have been considered "unclean" by Jewish tradition, a Canaanite mother. Even more importantly, she represented the historic enemy of the Children of Israel, the Canaanites.

> *Jesus left that place and went away to the district of Tyre and Sidon. Just then a Canaanite woman from that region came out and started shouting, "Have mercy on me, Lord, Son of David; my daughter is tormented by a demon. . . ." Then Jesus answered her, "Woman, great is your faith! Let it be done for you as you wish." And her daughter was healed instantly.*
> — MATTHEW 15:21-22; 28

For the Canaanite woman to approach Jesus speaks volumes of this mother's desperate plight to find peace for her daughter who was cruelly demon-possessed. Jesus had not invited the mother into a conversation with Him, but her desperation to overcome the evil which bound her daughter propelled her forward. The Canaanite mother cries out to Jesus, "Have mercy on me, Lord, Son of David; my daughter is tormented by a demon." The need for peacemaking is also personal!

Annoyed by the woman's behavior, Jesus' disciples urge Him to send the Canaanite away. Instead, Jesus listened to the woman and began a conversation with her. "'Woman, great is your faith! Let it be done for you as you wish.' And her daughter was healed instantly" (Matthew 15:28).

After this encounter with the Canaanite woman, we are told Jesus goes up a mountain where a large crowd comes to Him. The diseased and disabled are healed as the crowd marvels. The "God of

Israel" is praised. This expression of praise from the crowd, "the God of Israel," gives us the impression that, in this primarily Hellenistic area, this crowd is not of Israel.

The feeding of the 5,000 occurred after the beheading of John the Baptist. Rather than inciting the crowd to retaliate against the occupying Roman authorities, the current enemy of Israel, Jesus demonstrated another miracle of compassion. The feeding of the 4,000 occurred after His healing of the Canaanite mother's daughter (Matthew 15:32-38). Jesus exhibits compassion to those considered an unclean, historic enemy of Israel.

Peacemaking occurred.

Peacemaking of Early Friends — Mary Dyer and the "Gentle Invaders" of Friends Women

The Religious Society of Friends, or Friends Church, is one of the three historic peace churches in the United States: the Religious Society of Friends, the Church of the Brethren, and the Mennonites. From its beginnings during the English Reformation, Friends stood upon the peace testimony which was lived by Jesus Christ and embraced by the early New Testament church.

Eleven years after the death of her first husband, Margaret Fell and George Fox were married. By then Margaret was well seasoned in Friends theology and wrote the first public statement of the Friends peace testimony, which she delivered in 1660 to King Charles II, whose father had been executed during the English Reformation of the Church. She wanted to be clear and transparent about the identity of the Religious Society of Friends.

> We are a people that follow after those things that make for peace, love and unity. It is our desire that others' feet may walk in the same. [We] do deny and bear our testimony against all strife, wars, and contentions that come from the lusts that war in the members, that war against the soul, which we wait for, and watch for in all people. [We] love and desire the good of all. For no other cause but love to the souls of all people have our sufferings been.
>
> Therefore, have we been numbered amongst the transgressors and been accounted as sheep for the slaughter, as our Lord and

Master was, who is the captain of our salvation, who is gone before us, who though He was a Son, yet learned His obedience by the things He suffered who said, "My kingship is not of this world; if my kingship were of this world, my servants would fight . . . but my kingship is not from the world" (John 18:36). This is He that "came not to destroy men's lives but to save them" (Luke 9:56). This is He, that is our Lord and Master, whose testimony we must seal with our blood, if it be required of us. "For though we live in the world we are not carrying on a worldly war, for the weapons of our warfare are not worldly but have divine power to destroy strongholds" (2 Corinthians 10:3-4). . . .

Treason, treachery, and false dealings we do utterly deny — [and] false dealing, surmising, or plotting against any creature upon the face of the earth. We speak the truth in plainness and singleness of heart. All our desire is your good, peace, love and unity. This many thousands will seal with their blood, who are ready not only to believe, but to suffer, but only that the blood of the innocent many not come upon yourselves, through false information.[1]

Another Friends woman minister with an extraordinary and sacrificial witness to freedom and peace was Mary Dyer (1611-1660). Mary and her husband William emigrated from England in 1635 to the Massachusetts Bay Colony, where the concept of religious freedom did not include everyone. The early Puritan leaders wanted religious freedom from the state church of England with the ability to create their own colonial church regulations, thus limiting the religious freedom of others in their colony. When Mary returned to England in 1651, she met George Fox, became a convinced Friend, and eventually became a Friends minister.

Mary felt called to nonviolently challenge the laws which restricted religious freedoms. The leaders of the church in Boston had banned early Friends. If Quakers came to Boston and preached, they were stripped to the waist (both men and women), lashed, and abandoned to the border of the colony in the wilderness. Continued offenses resulted not just in imprisonment, but the removal of ears, having tongues gored, and finally death through public execution. Mary decided to join other early Friends witnessing for religious freedom from Boston's intolerant laws. On June 1, 1660, Mary was

Mary Dyer, by Sylvia Shaw Judson. Sculpture located in front of the Stout Meetinghouse at Earlham College campus, Richmond, Indiana.

hanged from an elm tree in Boston for her persistent witness. Her body hung as a "flag" for the freedom she sought. Since Mary had lived in Boston and was well known, her death at the hands of the religious leaders brought a response. The laws were changed.

Mary Dyer's execution in 1660 helped to set the foundation for American constitutional rights of religious freedom. A statue of Mary stands in front of the Massachusetts State House as a witness to her sacrifice. A plaque reads, "MY LIFE NOT AVAILETH ME IN COMPARISON TO THE LIBERTY OF THE TRUTH."[2] Such an important piece of American history should not be forgotten. Mary Dyer was a martyr and peacemaker for religious freedom.

During the later history of the United States, Friends worked to assist those desperately seeking freedom at all costs. In 1862, Western Yearly Meeting of Friends Church (WYM), in the state of Indiana, helped 2,799 people fleeing slavery. They furnished families with food, clothing, a copy of the Scriptures, and allowed children to attend the Friends schools. In 1864, they requested that the Indiana legislature appeal laws which divested individuals ". . . of their natural rights and which impair their evidence in courts of justice, and which embarrass their efforts in the cause of education."[3]

Well-known Friends active in this concern were Catharine and Levi Coffin, who provided aid to thousands fleeing bondage through the Underground Railroad, a loose system of abolitionist homes leading from the South to Northern states and Canada. Known as the president of the Underground Railroad, Levi and his wife Catharine eventually became members of Driftwood Friends Meeting of Western Yearly Meeting.

Linda B. Selleck, editor of this book and a recorded Friends minister, writes about the work of Friends who were members of Western Yearly Meeting and who witnessed against the violence of slavery in her book, *Gentle Invaders: Quaker Women Educators and Racial Issues During the Civil War and Reconstruction.*

> Western Yearly Meeting, established in 1858, comprised parts of Indiana and Illinois. From its beginnings this yearly meeting had a standing committee of concern over the status of blacks, and had done educational, evangelical and relief work before the war. Black

On the way to school: Students going to the Penn School on the Sea Islands of South Carolina.

children were invited to attend Quaker schools in areas where opportunities for black education were nonexistent.

In 1864 a new committee was formed by Western Friends to consider extensive relief work and around $10,000 was raised the first year. Eight teachers were sent to Clarkesville, Tennessee. Columbus, Mississippi was settled upon as Western's center of operation. Jonathan and Drusilla Wilson (a recorded minister), opened Mississippi schools along with twelve other teachers in November, 1866. One of the schools was set on fire, resulting in the death of an elderly black man. All of their equipment was lost but they continued their work until the next summer when the remaining teaching tools and equipment were stolen.

Western Yearly Meeting expanded its operations by supporting teachers in the mountains of Alabama at Mountain Home and Pratt's Mines. And, on the local front, the Refuge for Colored Children was opened at Indianapolis, Indiana, in 1871 under the direction of a dozen Quaker women, with Catherine Timberlake as matron, aided by funds from the yearly meeting.[4]

In the face of violence, Friends have advocated to overcome evil with good (Romans 12:14–21). As William Penn once said, "Let us see what love can do."

CHAPTER FOUR: PEACEMAKER

Arrow and Breath Prayers — First Steps of Peace

As we entered into our Cabrini ministry, Hope McDonald, the wife of a Young Life leader, knew how important it would be for me to develop a strong prayer life. She shared a copy of her book, *Discovering How to Pray*. In this book I learned about "arrow prayers." Arrow prayers help us to pray and walk in Christ Jesus throughout the day. Peacemaking needed to begin with me.

As we began ministry in Chicago, I spoke arrow prayers. When an ambulance with sirens blaring sped down Oak Street to Henrotin Hospital to transport a victim of a gang shooting, I prayed. On the days I went job hunting with a teen hoping to find a part-time job on Chicago's Near North Side, I prayed. As I went to visit Cabrini families and realized the elevator in the 500 W. Oak high-rise was not working and I would need to climb flights of graffiti-filled stairwells, I prayed for myself! Prayer allows us to turn over the challenges of life to the Lord so we do not carry them.

Arrow prayers can also be prayers of praise and thanksgiving. As I learned how to walk in the Spirit, I began to recognize the Lord's provisions and to allow the joy of the Lord to rise up in my heart. When an unexpected gift of money arrived to help cover an expense in ministry, I praised the Lord with an arrow prayer. When a young person arrived for the first time to our youth program, I would say, "Thank you, Jesus!" When the Lord helped me to find a parking spot and then park a fifteen-passenger van full of children on Cambridge Avenue without getting stuck in a frigid Chicago snowstorm, believe me, my heart was full of praise and thanksgiving! Arrow prayers help us to pray without ceasing (1 Thessalonians 5:17).

Historically the Church called short repetitive prayers "breath prayers." The Canaanite woman spoke a form of a breath prayer to Jesus, "Have mercy on me, Lord, Son of David" (breath in), "My daughter is cruelly demon-possessed" (breath out). In breath prayers we simply fall at the feet of the Living Christ in our hearts and cry for mercy. Rather than react violently to circumstances, we seek peace in our heart.

Once we have the peace of Christ Jesus in our hearts, it begins to spread to those close by. Sometimes it begins in small ways as we listen to what is happening around us and become involved. When Steve began the basketball teams, he had each participant sign a contract promising that they would stay in school, have their grades monitored by us, and attend weekly club meetings. No cursing or fighting were allowed. If students violated the rules, there were consequences and they could not play. New individual and peer habits occurred.

Having a church in the middle of Cabrini-Green was also an asset to peacemaking. One hot summer day, Steve noticed two groups of young men who were affiliated with two different gangs escalating a fight with each other on Oak Street. Grabbing a bucket from the Chicago Fellowship of Friends building, he went to the open fire hydrant, filled the bucket with water, and threw the water on the young men. Astonishingly, they left to grab their squirt guns and came back with their "soakers." What might have started a violent situation was redirected into fun.

One summer, the community churches began to organize volunteers to monitor the neighborhood playground during certain hours of the summer, so that mothers knew their children would be safe to play outside during those times. Peacemaking unfolds as we walk abiding in the "God of peace" (Romans 15:33).

How does prayer center you in peace and prepare you to work for peace in our world?

CHAPTER FIVE

Faith and Healing
Daughter

One of the cherished gifts I had from my mother was an aloe vera plant which stood in a sunny west window of our home. The original "mother" aloe vera plant was a gift from my grandmother to my mother. When I began my own home, my mother shared a start from the original plant with me. I have shared a start of this plant with my daughter. A succulent plant which can withstand irregular watering, the aloe vera is known for its healing capacity. It is my kind of plant!

Numerous times I broke off a piece of the aloe vera leaf in my home. The healing liquid from the leaf emerged and I spread it over a burnt finger of a child crying out in pain. I do not have a medical degree, but this plant seems to have a capacity to heal I do not possess. "It will be okay now," I would say to comfort my son or daughter. The plant is a treasure in my home.

To experience healing is *a simple joy!*

Daughter, Your Faith Has Made You Well

One of the numerous miracles performed by Jesus in the New Testament is the healing of a nameless woman who suffered a hemorrhage for twelve years (Mark 5:21–43). According to Jewish law, because of this condition she was considered unclean. In addition to the pain of her illness and the social isolation it caused, the woman "had endured much under many physicians" who had not helped at all. Abuse and poverty were added to her list of sufferings. She had lost so much and she was desperate! But this unknown woman had not lost hope. She heard Jesus was nearby.

In her heart, this chronically-ill woman had faith that Jesus would be different from the religious leaders who only condemned and isolated her. She believed He would be different from the physicians whose costly help only brought more suffering and despair. If she could touch the hem of Jesus' garment, she believed she would be healed (Mark 5:24b-30). Motivated by her faith, in her weak condition the suffering woman pressed through the crowd behind Jesus and touched His cloak as He passed by. She was immediately healed!

In the midst of the movement of people around Him, Jesus suddenly turned and stopped. He had been touched and power had been released. Jesus wanted to know the individual who had this unquestioning faith in Him.

Jesus turned and asked, "Who touched my clothes?" The disciples had no clue. The crowd pressed all around them. It could have been anyone!

Jesus persisted. His eyes searched for the person who had reached out in faith. The woman now realized she could not remain anony-

> *And a large crowd followed Him and pressed in on Him. Now there was a woman who had been suffering from hemorrhages for twelve years. She had endured much under many physicians, and had spent all that she had; and she was no better, but rather grew worse.*
>
> *She had heard about Jesus, and came up behind Him in the crowd and touched His cloak, for she said, "If I but touch His clothes, I will be made well." Immediately her hemorrhage stopped; and she felt in her body that she was healed of her disease.*
>
> *Immediately aware that power had gone forth from Him, Jesus turned about in the crowd and said, "Who touched my clothes? . . ."*
>
> *He said to her, "Daughter, your faith has made you well; Go in peace, and be healed of your disease."*
>
> — MARK 5:24b-30; 34

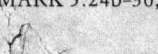

mous. Before everyone and with fear and trembling, she fell at the feet of Jesus, confessing she had indeed touched Him. The religious leaders believed the touch of an unclean person defiled them. Would Jesus also condemn her? To her amazement, He did not!

We are surprised that Jesus greets her affectionately as "Daughter," which is the same Greek word used by other gospel writers which include this healing (Matthew 9:20-22 and Luke 8:43-48). In the midst of a pressing crowd, Jesus had felt her fleeting touch, commended her faith, and healed her. She sought physical healing and received so much more — His recognition and commendation, compassionate care, peace, and freedom from suffering!

Our willingness to proclaim our experience of healing through Christ Jesus is a great ministry to others. Through the sharing of our woundedness, search for healing, and restoration, our witness of faith increases the faith of others who need healing. Our "test" becomes a testimony; our "mess" becomes our message. We let our lives speak hope to those in need!

It is interesting that the healing of this "Daughter" by Jesus, as recounted in the Gospel of Mark, is intermixed with a different account — the healing of the young daughter of Jairus, a leader in the synagogue (Mark 5:21-24; 35-43). Jairus seeks out Jesus in a large crowd, falls at His feet, and implores Jesus to come and place His healing hands on the dying child that she might live. But as they prepare to leave, the bleeding woman reaches Jesus, touching and drawing His healing power into her. As that encounter ends, some people from Jairus' home appear with the news of his daughter's death, and tell the devastated father not to bother Jesus anymore.

Jesus now ministers to Jairus, telling the stricken father to ignore their report, and encourages him to have faith. "Do not fear, only believe."

Jairus' lesson on faith would not be easy. Upon his return home, people had already gathered to grieve and cry loudly upon the death of his daughter. When Jesus attempts to speak faith to these "friends," the group just laughs. There is no faith to be found in this crowd who seem intent upon pulling Jairus into their emotional well of grief.

In order for the second daughter's miracle to occur, Jesus removes all who lack faith from Jairus' home. With the girl's parents and a few of Jesus' disciples in the room, He takes the twelve-year-old by the hand, and the girl stands up. In this chapter of Mark, we have the healing of TWO daughters and an amazing witness to the importance of faith.

Have You Ever Been Desperate for a Healing?

Many people today need the healing touch of Jesus Christ for so many aspects of their lives. They are in physical and/or emotional pain. They are in spiritual pain and mental confusion. They suffer social condemnation. They have lost their personal resources. They need peace.

To encounter the healing touch of Jesus, you must seek Him and reach out in faith.

In today's world of secular humanism, we are not encouraged to seek God. We seek to associate with others who share our pain . . . we seek to medicate our pain . . . we seek "experts" in the field of our concern. When we reach the end of our own resources, we often begin to despair and lose hope. Without the basic message of faith and hope, prayer for spiritual healing is too often forgotten.

I once heard a sermon that compared our churches today to hospitals. Today if bleeding people sought out medical attention and were left on a gurney in the hallway, they would sue the institution for malpractice. Nevertheless, too often people who are wounded spiritually come to our churches and we do nothing for their healing. Where are the spiritually prepared elders of the church, equipped with profound faith to administer prayers of healing, restoration, and wholeness into the wounded lives of others?

Elizabeth Hooton and Ann Branson

To hear today's stories of healing among Friends one must often speak to people personally. In one-on-one conversations with individuals within the Friends Church, the deeper spiritual life can be

CHAPTER FIVE: FAITH AND HEALING

The Message, by J. Walter West (1860-1933). Note that the woman standing to speak from the ministers and elders bench has placed her bonnet on the wall peg behind her.

heard. The private stories of those who have experienced dramatic healing from the Lord are often not recorded.

However, during the first generation of the Friends movement, founder George Fox kept a record of a great many accounts that revealed God's presence and power in the ministry of Fox and other Friends. He left behind money to publish this collection after his death in 1691, but the original manuscript was lost. In 1932 Quaker scholar Henry Cadbury discovered a catalogue in the London Friends Library which cited the miracles attributed to George Fox. Cadbury's edition of Fox's *Book of Miracles* was first published in 1948, and was republished by Friends United Press in 2000. Both editions recount 150 miracle stories of the power of the Living Christ at work in early Friends.

Early miracles among Friends included those experienced through Elizabeth Hooton's ministries (1600-1672). "She began her work in 1648 and was therefore the first woman to preach the Truth as expressed by George Fox. She endured terrible persecutions in New England with marked fortitude."[1] In the *First Publishers of Truth*, issued by London Yearly Meeting of Friends in 1676,

Elizabeth is listed as one of the "Valiant Sixty" Friends ministers from Nottinghamshire, England; the first woman to be recorded as a Friends minister.

Elizabeth traveled widely in Friends ministry even at an old age. During her trip to New England, Elizabeth's healing ministry was evidenced.

> And when I came to the east parts of New England the Lord wrought great things by me there, and many came in amongst us, that the meeting at the eastward way increased much whilst I was with them and the hand of the Lord was with me, praises to his name forever, both in outward miracles and in the work of the Spirit. One woman that had been convinced was nigh unto death that none thought she could have lived, and when the doctor had left her and given her up for dead then was I made glad that so they might see the power of God above the doctor and all outward physicians. So, the Lord raised her up by his own power from that very time and she became a fine Friend.
>
> There was another woman that was no Friend that was nigh unto death, and when many people of the world were about her looking when she should depart this life and her husband and family crying, I was made to go amongst them to the woman that was nigh death, and when I had kneeled down to pray with her, her spirit revived from that same time, and the Lord healed her and all the people saw it and said it was the Lord's work. And this woman was after a fine and a tender-hearted woman, who much loved me, and several that saw it praised God and came to meetings; so that the blessing of God was upon the eastern parts; several great men came; so, the word of God was prospered.[2]

Elizabeth prayed for healing and worked to heal conditions of need. She let her life speak.

As a teenager, Ann Branson (1808–1891) heard an English Friends minister, Elizabeth Robson, preach at her meeting in Flushing, Ohio. Ann began to struggle with a call to ministry. Years later another Friends woman minister visited Ann, who was ill, and felt Ann's respiratory infection was like the young man who lacked the one thing, "that of selling all and following the Lord Jesus in the way of his requiring (Mark 10:17-21)." Ann wrote in her *Journal* (10th month, 1833):

> Thus, the Lord let me see and feel that man of himself can do nothing — he cannot soften his own heart, he cannot repent when he pleases and become resigned to the will of the Lord in his own will and time. I had chosen my own way and disobeyed his command, when a clear manifestation of religious duty had been given me and strength to comply therewith, and now I was reaping the reward of disobedience. This was the condition of my mind, when, one day after a severe spell of coughing, I sank for a few moments into a state of unconsciousness.... Then this language was addressed to my spiritual ear, "Art thou now willing to become a little preacher?"
>
> I answered, "Lord, thou hast all power. I have no might or strength of my own, make of me what seems unto thee good...."
>
> I now felt that resignation to the will of the Lord which I once thought impossible. Under this feeling to humiliation of self, this language was addressed to the ear of my soul, "Fear not, for I am with thee; be not dismayed, for I am thy God" (Isaiah 41:10). No tongue could tell, or pen portray, the joy of my heart at that time. I felt that all my sins were forgiven through the mercy of God in Christ Jesus, and a foretaste of that joy which is unspeakable and full of glory (I Peter 1:8) was given me — a foretaste of joys of heaven....
>
> I was now commanded of the Lord to send for the inhabitants of the village near which we resided, that I might proclaim unto them the unsearchable riches of Christ.... They were invited to come, taste, and see that the Lord is good and that his mercy endures forever, that it is extended unto all, that He is no respecter of persons, that in every nation they that fear Him and work righteousness are accepted with Him.... But we must come in the obedience of faith — we must follow the leadings and teachings of the Holy Spirit, whilst favored with the visitation of Divine mercy, the mercy of God in Christ Jesus our Lord and Savior, if we become heirs of eternal salvation. Christ Jesus came not into the world to suffer and to die for us, to save us in our sins, but *from* our sins. We must experience the refining, cleansing operation of His baptism — the baptism of fire and Holy Ghost, purging the temple of our

hearts from all that His righteous controversy is with, before He will deign to own us before His Father and the holy angels. . . . From this time I began slowly to recover. . . .³

Testimonies of Healing

Grandmothers can have a compelling and influential spiritual witness in the lives of their grandchildren. When I was a child, my grandmother Ruth Molloy shared a powerful witness of healing faith in her own life which has been an inspiration to me.

When my grandmother gave birth to my mother, she soon knew something was seriously wrong. Her newborn could not hold down milk and became so thin and frail that her hands "looked like a bird's foot." The inability to gain nourishment meant her infant would only wail from the pain of starvation. Soon my grandmother was distraught at what to do to help her daughter. She had already lost one child at birth and had tried everything she knew to bring little Glenna Jean relief. Realizing the gravity of the situation, my grandfather drove their perilously ill babe to the nearest hospital, in Marshalltown, Iowa, for help.

My exhausted grandmother knelt at the side of her bed to pray. She had tried everything she knew to bring her newborn relief. And as she prayed, my grandmother sensed a divine presence of light fill the room. She heard Christ speak to her that all would be well. God's peace filled her and she got up and went to sleep.

Yes, Grandmother's daughter was healed! Upon reaching the hospital, the doctors did not know what was wrong but were willing to do emergency surgery to see if they could find an answer. Doing nothing would mean sure death. Their surgery revealed a stomach blockage. Correcting the blockage returned life to the little one. My grandparents' daughter — my mother — was healed.

Members of my family have repeated this witness to each generation. We have been taught that we are loved by the Lord and He is a Living God still capable of intervening in miraculous ways in our lives. Over the years I have received my own testimony of this reality.

CHAPTER FIVE: FAITH AND HEALING

Steve and Marlene Pedigo.

When Steve and I began ministry with the Chicago Fellowship of Friends we became foster parents to fourteen-year-old Donald, who had shot another teen from a rival gang in Cabrini. Rather than incarceration, the judge sentenced him to live with us as an alternative to imprisonment. Steve joked he didn't know which was worse — jail or living with us!

We had just acquired the St. Philip of Benzini Catholic School as our new Chicago Fellowship of Friends site. It was in need of MAJOR renovation. Steve was away at a summer camp with teens, so I asked Donald to help me take debris to the dumpster in back of the building. As we started our work project, I suddenly heard a commotion on the sidewalk. I rushed outside to discover Donald surrounded by members of the opposite gang, armed with bats and bricks initiating a fight with him. With a holy boldness I did not realize I possessed, I rushed to Donald's side and demanded that the startled group leave at once or I would call the police. As they left, a member of the gang threw a brick aiming to hit Donald. As I extended my arm to protect him, the brick struck my right hand.

The next day being Sunday, the Chicago Fellowship of Friends was meeting for worship at our new site at 515 West Oak. With Steve gone, I had planned to play the piano, lead worship, and preach. As

I sat at the piano my eyes filled with tears as I realized two fingers were swollen and not moving — I prayed for a miracle.

Suddenly, my fingers could move — I was healed! Not only was I able to move forward with music, but I shared this powerful testimony with the gathered group during my message. I will never forget the encouragement of Mrs. Thornton, one of the Cabrini row house saints, who said that the Lord had granted me the gift of this dynamic vocal ministry as a witness and encouragement for our church, as we were just beginning to settle into our new building and location.

Stories of faith, prayer, and healing are powerful testimonies not just in the New Testament, but also in the church today. Do we know daughters or sons in our present lives who need healing?

Do you have a testimony?

CHAPTER SIX

A Transformed Life Transforms Others
The Anointing Woman

New beginnings are a wonderful celebration. My extended family has been celebrating the birth of babies recently. One summer when I went home to Iowa to see everyone, I realized a new generation had announced their presence in our family system as little ones ruled in the house. Babies, toddlers, and preschoolers bring new energy and charm their way into the hearts of all the family. It is a tremendous season of life for praise and thanksgiving.

Spiritual births are also a time of praise and celebration. There is something about a new Christian who "gets it" and "lives it" that energizes the church around them. Hearing the testimonies of those who have been transformed through Christ inspires and revives us all. God's love just seems to spill out of their hearts of praise. It is contagious!

One of the New Testament women who demonstrated how personal transformation motivates service and transforms others was the anonymous anointing woman (Luke 7:36-50).

Simon the Pharisee and the Anointing Woman

One day, Simon the Pharisee invited Jesus to eat with him at his home. The Pharisees were frequently in dialogue with Jesus about His teachings. We are told little about Simon's faith in Jesus, only that he initially referred to Jesus as Rabbi or Teacher (Luke 7:40). As was often the case with Jesus, His most powerful teachings came not from arguing over the Jewish law, but rather from the opportunities for ministry through His parables and probing queries.

Although Simon had invited Jesus to dinner, he had neglected the customary acts of hospitality. It seems there had been no wel-

> [Jesus said:] "A certain creditor had two debtors; one owed five hundred denarii, and the other fifty. When they could not pay, he canceled the debts for both of them. Now which of them will love him more?"
>
> Simon answered, "I suppose the one for whom he canceled the greater debt."
>
> And Jesus said to him, "You have judged rightly."
>
> Then turning toward the woman, he said to Simon, "Do you see this woman? I entered your house; you gave me no water for my feet, but she has bathed my feet with her tears and dried them with her hair. You gave me no kiss, but from the time I came in she has not stopped kissing my feet. You did not anoint my head with oil, but she has anointed my feet with ointment. Therefore, I tell you, her sins, which were many, have been forgiven; hence she has shown great love. But the one to whom little is forgiven, loves little."
>
> Then He said to her, "Your sins are forgiven."
>
> —LUKE 7:41–48

coming kiss, no oil for the dry and wind-swept hair on Jesus' head, and no washing of His dusty feet. Suddenly Simon's dinner plans are interrupted by an unexpected woman who anoints Jesus' head, washes His feet with her tears, and covers His feet with her hair and kisses. What kind of vulgar, unseemly display was this for religious leaders having dinner together? Simon's response demonstrated that he knew exactly what kind of woman was in his home. Jesus wasn't a real prophet or He would have known the true nature of that woman and her outrageous and unseemly familiarity with Jesus. The interrupted dinner provided an important teachable moment.

The actions of this anointing woman, described as a "sinner," imparts a powerful spiritual lesson. Her courageous and extravagant actions poured out upon Jesus in love and gratitude stand in sharp contrast to the lapse of welcoming hospitality by Simon. As this scene unfolded, Jesus told

CHAPTER SIX: A TRANSFORMED LIFE TRANSFORMS OTHERS

a parable about the reality of repentance, redemption, and gratitude (Luke 7:41-50). He said to the woman, "Your sins are forgiven." Some Christian scholars believe this nameless woman is Mary of Bethany.

Today we may smile and think we would not have condemned this woman. However, when it comes to our approach to "those" who are different than "us," we often exhibit a spirit of shunning condemnation reflected in the existing homogeneous demographics of our church. Sometimes we embrace a "cancel culture" mentality. The early Friends rejected the Calvinist belief that certain individuals were predestined to the Kingdom of God. They believed all people were created in God's image and able to respond to the Holy Spirit. Thus, the early Friends were known for their missionary zeal to all people, even those who were rejected by society. How do we help people today break the enslaving chains in their lives, and encourage them to rise to new life through Christ Jesus? How do we share our faith with others?

Elizabeth Fry, "The Angel of Prisons"

A recorded Friends minister who courageously cared for people and changed the lives of prisoners in her country was Elizabeth Fry (1780-1845). In an era when English prisons resembled degenerate dungeons and children were locked away with their parents, Elizabeth's transformed spiritual life and extraordinary prison reforms made a profound difference and changed countless lives for women and men in England and eventually throughout Europe, as her reform movement spread.

On February 4, 1798, seventeen-year-old Elizabeth sat in the Norwich Friends meeting for worship wearing her "smart" purple boots with scarlet laces under her dress. That day Elizabeth heard a traveling Friends minister, William Savery, preach on salvation and the joy the Lord would bring to a repentant heart. Tears fell as the Holy Spirit spoke to her. Elizabeth asked her father to invite the minister to their home for a meal so she could talk more with William. Her life changed dramatically.

Elizabeth Fry.

CHAPTER SIX: A TRANSFORMED LIFE TRANSFORMS OTHERS

Elizabeth wrote in her journal of this experience: ". . . in short, what he [William Savery] said and what I felt, was like a refreshing shower falling upon earth, that had been dried up for ages. It has not made me unhappy: I have felt ever since humble. I have longed for virtue."[1] Elizabeth soon embraced the Friends plainness of speech and dress. Her sister, Richenda, wrote of Elizabeth:

> Betsy's character is certainly, in many respects, extremely improved, since she has adopted these principles. She is industrious, charitable to the poor, kind and attentive to all of us; in short, if it was not for that serious manner which Quakerism throws over a person, Betsy would indeed be a most improved character. . . .
>
> The Bible became her study, visiting the poor, especially the sick, her great object. We were too ignorant ourselves to know what the workings of her mind were, but we could discover the most marked change in her. To us she was now always amiable and patient, forbearing and humble. And in looking back upon the change in her life, and its great results, we may feel assured that God was at work in her soul, and that she was really and truly awakening to a new life in Christ Jesus.[2]

As a teenager, Elizabeth began to organize Bible studies on Sunday afternoons for the poor children in her community. This compassion for the poor remained in her heart even after she married Joseph Fry and started a family. As a young mother, she continued to give to the needy, and then opened her Bible to read and pray with those who gathered.

In 1813, Stephen Grellet, a refugee from the French Revolution and a recorded American Friends minister, made his way to England and met with Elizabeth. He challenged her to visit Newgate Prison, known as "hell above ground." At that time Newgate Prison was the home of four to five hundred women and their children — a crowded, unsanitary prison known for its cursing, gambling, and drinking. Prisons were mostly dungeons of punishment and severe deprivation, rather than places of reform.

Elizabeth made her first visit to Newgate Prison with her sister, Hannah Gurney Buxton, in 1813. The women were appalled at the conditions they found, and deeply moved when many of the Newgate

Mrs. Fry Reading to the Prisoners in Newgate in the Year 1816. Photo print made by Thomas Oldham Barlow of the painting by Jerry Barrett (1824-1906).

women knelt around them. On a subsequent visit, Elizabeth read to the women the parable of the vineyard from the Bible, and spoke to them of Christ having come to save those who had wasted their lives by being estranged from Him. In 1817, after a few years of regular visits, receiving wise counsel, and prayerfully seeking the Lord's guidance, Elizabeth spoke to the Newgate mothers about organizing a school for their children. The Sheriffs of London, the Ordinary, and the Governor of Newgate gave permission for her to use an unoccupied cell. Thus, Elizabeth began her work of faith and labor of love.[3]

In April of 1817, a committee of women also became active at the prison — the "Association for the Improvement of the Female Prisoners in Newgate." They intended to "provide for the clothing, the instruction, and the employment of the women; to introduce them to a knowledge of the Holy Scriptures, and to form in them, as much as possible, those habits of order, sobriety and industry, which may render them docile and peaceable whilst in prison, and respectable when they leave it."[4] During the first month, the women of this committee devoted themselves to their task at Newgate Prison and "... almost lived amongst them. At first, every day in the week, and every hour in the day, found some of them there, joining in the work or instructing the pupils, from the time they dressed to the close of the day."[5]

Magistrates believed that the Newgate women prisoners would not submit to the women of the committee. Mrs. Fry's answer was, "Let the experiment be tried."[6] The prison was cleaned, the women were clothed, the children were in school, and the women were taught the Bible and given the opportunity to work. Queen Victoria granted Elizabeth several audiences, admired her efforts, and supported the work financially. Elizabeth's transformed life transformed others in Newgate Prison, and later, prisoners in other countries. ***The experiment had been tried and succeeded!***

Elizabeth (Rous) Comstock

A second Friends woman minister who was active in prison ministry was Elizabeth Comstock (1815-1891). Born in Berkshire, England, to a Friends family, Elizabeth's mother took her, at the age of eight, to the London Yearly Meeting of the Religious Society of Friends where she had the opportunity to hear Elizabeth Fry speak.

> I shall never forget the impression she made upon my young mind by her sweet voice, beautiful face, and her earnest pleading, as she spoke of the prisoners, the suffering and the outcast. I was too young to understand one half of what she said, yet good seed was sown then and there, which led to active labor in after years. In the solemn silence that followed, after she took her seat, my childish heart was lifted in the prayer that I might grow as good as she was, and work in the same way. Although an unusually wild, willful and playful child, yet in my most sacred and secret moments, I returned to the prayer of my childhood, and these impressions were deepened every time I had the privilege of seeing and hearing her in after years.[7]

Later in life, Elizabeth moved to Michigan, married John T. Comstock, and became recorded in ministry by Indiana Yearly

Elizabeth L. Comstock.

Meeting. After meeting President Lincoln, Elizabeth visited one of the largest Union Army prisoners-of-war camps, Camp Douglas, on the south side of Chicago, Illinois. Deplorable conditions at the Confederate Prison Camp resulted in a death rate of 17% to 28%. A mass grave of 4,275 Confederate prisoners still exists in Chicago's Oak Wood Cemetery. While in Chicago, Elizabeth gathered the first Friends meeting in the city, the Chicago Monthly Meeting (WYM).

CHAPTER SIX: A TRANSFORMED LIFE TRANSFORMS OTHERS

This was the same meeting that Ron and Linda Selleck (my book editor) pastored from 1980-1984. Elizabeth visited prisoner-of-war camps and wrote about her findings to the Secretary of War, Edwin M. Stanton. She also worked with Laura Smith Haviland, who with her husband started the first racially integrated school in Michigan. They were staunch abolitionists and their home was a part of the Underground Railroad.

Other Friends women shared the concern for prison reform. Rhoda Coffin, another recorded Friends minister, helped to establish the first women's adult correctional facility in Indianapolis, Indiana, in 1873. Jane Addams, from a prominent Illinois Quaker family, became the second woman to be awarded the Nobel Peace Prize, in 1931. Her pioneering social work helped to establish the Juvenile Protection Association, in 1901, which led to the first juvenile court in the US. Quakerdale in Iowa and Josiah White's in Indiana, large child welfare not-for-profits, also sprang from the Friends concern for children. From the witness of thousands of seventeenth-century Friends who suffered imprisonment and even death for the cause of religious freedom in England emerged extraordinary Friends women and men of later generations, who provided ministries and relief to countless incarcerated individuals and labored to improve many prison systems and for other social reforms.

Transformational Ministry

As Steve and I began our outreach ministry, Cabrini-Green was one of the oldest public housing developments in the city of Chicago. Over 20,000 residents called Cabrini-Green's three-by-five-block area their home: three-fourths of the residents were twenty-one years of age and younger. The Near North Side of Chicago had been the site of generational poverty for decades, as various immigrant groups were drawn there in search of employment and then moved on to other communities in the metropolitan area once their families were established.

By the 1950s and 1960s new high-rise public housing was meant to improve the expanding web of social problems which

The Chicago Fellowship of Friends, by Lucy Sikes.

had developed — unemployment, illiteracy, high rates of teenage pregnancy, child abuse/neglect, substance abuse, and gang violence. However, this was an ill-planned attempt to contain generational poverty in densely populated youth-filled public housing. Existing crime and teen gangs seemed only to provide a tinderbox for the acceleration of chaos and abuse in the lives of the young residents of Cabrini. Too many mothers in the Cabrini community faced tears and heartbreak, grief, and sorrow, as violence erupted as abruptly in these apartment buildings as a summer storm.

After the murder of Dr. Martin Luther King, Jr., businesses which lost property during the riots that followed often took their insurance money and relocated to the suburbs. It was not uncommon for churches to flee to these newer communities, and then send money to fresh new not-for-profits which developed. A separation between the message of the church of Jesus Christ and fundraising to finance "good deeds" occurred. Too often members of churches did not want to become involved personally in the systemic failure of institutions which remained in urban poor communities.

Shortly after we began the Chicago Fellowship of Friends ministry under the care of Chicago Monthly Meeting (WYM), and

CHAPTER SIX: A TRANSFORMED LIFE TRANSFORMS OTHERS

as a mission project of Friends United Meeting, we were approached by a local probation officer to become foster parents for Cabrini teens as an alternative to incarceration. As we took the troubled youths into our home, I realized many of them had been under the care of the Illinois Department of Children and Family Services (DCFS) for abuse and/or neglect. Although the children were returned to their homes, conditions really had not improved. They merely were passed on to Juvenile Court of Cook County for the next stage of government care. I could not understand why intervention did not consider the best interest of the child, but soon realized that federal funding was tied to family reunification. States made money as they returned a child home, even if they had to return the child home several times.

I worked with other Cook County foster mothers to strengthen the rights of children and foster parents in the State of Illinois, and to improve the conditions in the community surrounding the Chicago Fellowship of Friends to prevent children slipping into conditions of abuse and neglect. Accordingly, we taught principles of peace and violence prevention in the youth and children's programs we developed at the Chicago Fellowship of Friends.

Our meetinghouse was not merely used on Sundays for worship, but was open throughout the week and year-round as a safe haven for children and youth. Not only did we build relationships with these young ones as they grew to adulthood, but our time of ministry in Cabrini-Green lasted long enough for us to begin ministry to the children of the youth we had first met in the 1970s. Lives changed. The transformation we sought was more than successful program development that showed statistical success for funders. It was a discernment of "wrap around" ministry. A substantial Friends church emerged from this youth ministry, the Chicago Fellowship of Friends.

Has the Lord given you an "experiment to be tried?"

CHAPTER SEVEN

Deacon, Minister, Apostle
Mary Magdalene and the Ministering Women

As I travel in the ministry, I often hear a religious syncretism which advocates love God and others. If you are a woman, that "melting pot" theology of globalization is not experienced equally. There is a tremendous difference in the status and treatment of women in the world's faith traditions.

In the pulpits of the church today there is too often a vacuum when it comes to lifting up the stories of New Testament women involved in ministry. In many of our communities, we have also forgotten the role of women in American history. Let us start to analyze the "glass ceiling" of the church and examine why women are too often relegated to certain categories or tasks in ministry, rather than released as faithful women called and led by the Holy Spirit to preach the full gospel of Jesus Christ as ministers. Within New Testament Christianity and the history of the Religious Society of Friends, there is a precious legacy of women in ministry which needs proclamation.

It is time.

Mary Magdalene and the Ministering Women

When someone begins to say, "Women are to be silent in the church," my first defense is often to share about Mary Magdalene, whose life proclaims the core message of Christianity. Her witness starts with the reality that through the restoration available in Christ Jesus, we can receive deliverance and forgiveness from sin and evil, and thus walk in communion with the Lord. Secondly, Mary Magdalene is a woman who worked in community with other women in the early emerging role of deacon in the church. Finally, in the ministry of Mary Magdalene we meet the first individual commissioned by

CHAPTER SEVEN: DEACON, MINISTER, APOSTLE

Christ Jesus to proclaim to the disciples the Good News of the Resurrection, "an apostle to the apostles." The witness of Mary Magdalene is not one of silence, but a powerful reminder of transformation through a living relationship with Christ Jesus — an example of a woman in ministry.

The gospel writer Luke gives us a glimpse into the identity of Mary Magdalene. Although introductions of ministers today often do not speak of deliverance from evil, Luke reveals that Mary Magdalene had experienced deliverance from seven demons! If you have

> *And it came to pass afterward, that he went throughout every city and village, preaching and shewing the glad tidings of the kingdom of God: and the twelve were with Him. And certain women, which had been healed of evil spirits and infirmities, Mary called Magdalene, out of whom went seven devils, and Joanna the wife of Chuza Herod's steward, and Susanna, and many others, which ministered unto Him of their substance.*
>
> — LUKE 8:1-3, KING JAMES VERSION, 1611

known the bondage of addiction, the pain of emotional wounds, or the trauma of violence, you realize how powerful it is to say you have experienced healing. A personal testimony is hard to discount or dismiss. A testimony of deliverance from "seven demons" would be powerful. Although we do not know the details of the demons of Mary Magdalene, we are told she had experienced a powerful release from bondage and restoration to a rightly ordered mind and spirit.

Mary Magdalene's personal experience of divine deliverance compelled her to choose a life of service to Jesus Christ. The Greek verb used to describe this in Luke 8:3 is *diakoneo*, a ministry of a service motivated by love, translated as "ministered" in the King James Version of the Bible. *Diakonos* was nearly absent from the Old Testament and the Greeks did not believe service was dignified. It was Christ Jesus who elevated Christian service to be a mark of true discipleship and reversed what were then considered to be lowly and inferior actions. Hermann Beyer writes in the *Theological Dictionary of the New Testament*,

> Jesus' view of service grows out of the OT command of love for one's neighbor, which He takes and links with the command of love for God to constitute the substance of the divinely willed ethical conduct of His followers. In so doing, He purifies the concept of service from the distortions which it had suffered in Judaism. Jesus' attitude to service is completely new as compared with the Greek understanding. The decisive point is that He sees in it the thing which makes a man His disciple. . . .
>
> Jesus comprises under the term *diakonein* many different activities such as giving food and drink, extending shelter, providing clothes and visiting the sick and prisoners. The term thus comes to have the full sense of active Christian love for the neighbor and as such it is a mark of true discipleship of Jesus. For what the Christian does to even the least of his fellowmen he does to the Lord Himself.[1]

Mary Magdalene and the ministering women named and described by Luke give us a glimpse into this developing role in the church. Paul describes the primary tasks of New Testament deacons in 1 Timothy 3:8-13. Later the word *diakonos* was used by Paul to describe Phoebe, the deaconess of the church of Cenchreae (Romans 16:1). Phoebe was entrusted by Paul to deliver the epistle of Romans. An order of deaconesses in the early church quickly developed as a symbol of loving care for others.

The faithful service of Mary Magdalene and the ministering women can be found recorded not only during the ministry of Jesus Christ, but at the death of Jesus on the cross (Mark 15:40) and at the tomb (Luke 24:10). Mary Magdalene's decisions to stay with Jesus' mother at the foot of the cross throughout the unspeakable tortures of the crucifixion, and to be a ministering presence at His tomb, were diametrically opposite Peter's betrayal of Jesus and his absence at the cross.

A third aspect of the ministry of Mary Magdalene is detailed in John 20:11-18, as the Risen Christ commissions and releases her to proclaim the message of His Resurrection to the disciples. More than pronouncing the central message of Christ's resurrection, this passage shows women of faith elevated by Christ Himself to proclaim the Good News of the gospel, when so led by the Holy Spirit. His radical commissioning of Mary Magdalene stands in stark contrast to the role and place at that time of women in Greek and Jewish societies, which did not consider women to be legal or valid witnesses.

Western Yearly Meeting
Historic Friends Women in the Ministry

In 2005, my husband and I became Co-Superintendents of Western Yearly Meeting of Friends Church, located in the western section of Indiana and the eastern portion of Illinois. I was surprised to learn of the number of women recorded in the ministry in Western's history, beginning as far back as 1858, when this Yearly Meeting was first gathered as a church, and before its pastoral system was established.

1858 RECORDED WOMEN MINISTERS OF WESTERN YEARLY MEETING

Blue River Quarterly Meeting (*out of seven ministers, five were women*): Martha Wilson, Jane Trueblood, Amy Moore, Mary Stevens, and Mary Newby.

White Lick Quarterly Meeting (*out of eight ministers, three were women*): Hannah B. Tatum, Ann Mills, and Ann Hoskins.

Western Quarterly Meeting (*out of three ministers, one was a woman*): Dorcas Hunt.

Union/Westfield Quarterly Meeting (*out of six ministers, three were women*): Asenath Clark, Esther Carson, Sarah Hiatt.

Concord Quarterly Meeting (*out of four ministers, one was a woman*): Mary Ann Rich.

1908 RECORDED WOMEN MINISTERS OF WESTERN YEARLY MEETING

Bloomingdale Quarterly Meeting (*out of fourteen ministers, six were women*): Sarah J. Lindley, Sarah T. McKay, Sarah M. Woodard, Alice A. Mendenhall, Diantha C. Martin, and, DeElla Leonard.

Blue River Quarterly Meeting (*out of nine ministers, two were women*): Eunice Furnas and Lucinda Cadle.

Carmel Quarterly Meeting (*out of nine ministers, five were women*): Lavina Weaver, Carrie M. Henderson, Flora Holiday, Sarah J. King, and Gertrude Moon Reinier.

Chicago Quarterly Meeting (*out of eleven ministers, four were women*): Rhoda M. Coffin, Charlotte E. Vickers, Sarah A. Kelsey, and Hannah S. Wing.

Danville Quarterly Meeting (*out of five ministers, one was a woman*): Sarah M. Hadley.

Fairfield Quarterly Meeting (*out of five ministers, none were women*).

Kokomo Quarterly Meeting (*out of seventeen ministers, six were women*): Charlotte Van Bibber, Rebecca Ruth Ellis, Josephine Hockett, Mary Emily Ellis, Mary V. Couch, and Rachel E. Thomas.

New London Quarterly Meeting (*out of ten ministers, two were women*): Rachel Binford and Phoebe A. Littler.

Plainfield Quarterly Meeting (*out of eighteen ministers, six were women*): Mary A. Cox, Eliza C. Armstrong, Rebecca Flagler, Hannah Pratt Jessup, Emeline H. Tuttle, and Nancy Duffy.

Pleasant Grove Quarterly Meeting (*out of four ministers, one was a woman*): Ruth S. Green.

Sand Creek Quarterly Meeting (*out of six ministers, two were women*): Phoebe A. Cox and Elizabeth P. Milhous.

Thorntown Quarterly Meeting (*out of four ministers, one was a woman*): Martha J. Binford.

Vermilion Quarterly Meeting (*out of nineteen ministers, five were women*): Martha Underwood, Martilia Cox, Melissa S. Haworth, Goldie E. Thompson, and Martha E. Barber.

West Grove Quarterly Meeting (*out of eight ministers, one was a woman*): Lydia E. Carson.

Westfield Quarterly Meeting (*out of sixteen ministers, four were women*): Anna Tomlinson, Mary N. Cox, Myriam Symons, and Elizabeth Murphy.

White Lick Quarterly Meeting (*out of eight ministers, three were women*): Rebecca H. Macy, Ruth Ellen Guyer, and Lydia Taylor Painter.

— *Semi-Centennial Anniversary of Western Yearly Meeting of Friends Church*.[2]

CHAPTER SEVEN: DEACON, MINISTER, APOSTLE

By 1908, many WYM churches had recorded women in the ministry who provided pastoral ministry. Some worked and traveled in the ministry with their husbands who were also recorded ministers. Hinkle Creek Friends in Hamilton County, Indiana, had eight women who served in ministry during a one-hundred-year period. Following are brief descriptions of the ministries of some of the recorded Friends women ministers from Hamilton County, from the time Western Yearly Meeting began in 1858 through the twentieth century:

Asenath (Hunt) [1785-1872] and Dougan Clark (Eagle Creek/Greenwood Friends)

Asenath was recorded a minister of the Gospel in North Carolina in 1817, when about thirty-two years of age. We have in her a remarkable example of patient and continued labor. She was seldom without a minute for service, visiting and traveling largely east and west within the limits of nearly or quite all the yearly meetings on this continent, as well as an extended visit of nineteen months, in company with her husband, Dougan Clark, a minister, in England and Ireland. . . . Her ministry was sound in doctrine and edifying in character; her warnings solemn and at times peculiarly impressive, yet always clothed in language of persuasive tenderness and encouragement; her exhortations warm, tender and well adapted to draw her hearers to Christ. The young, as well as the old, ever found in her a friend that could understand their spiritual needs, and could sympathize with them in their trials and temptations. Being well instructed in the things of the Kingdom of God, she was often enabled to bring forth from her treasury things new and old.[3]

Asenath and Dougan served as the first Superintendents of New Garden Friends Boarding School for five years, which eventually became known as Guilford College, located in Greensboro, North Carolina. Their son Dougan Clark was an early professor of religion at Earlham College in Richmond, Indiana, and authored the book, *The Theology of Holiness*. (Clark, a doctor, practiced medicine for fifteen years before moving to Richmond.)

Esther (Beals) Carson [1807-1883] (Hinkle Creek/West Grove)

A minister past middle age. Character of her ministry that of exhortation. A good woman and faithful.[4]

Eunice Furnas [1841–1917] (Spicewood Friends)

While still a girl she might often have been seen by the light of a tallow candle in her father's house in the upper room reading the Word of God. Under these conditions there came a knowledge of her birth into the Kingdom of Christ and a clear conception of the task which was to be hers to perform. She was recorded minister of the Gospel in 1874 by Spicewood Monthly Meeting, West Grove Quarterly Meeting. In these two meetings, most of her active ministry was performed.... For one year she labored in Mountain Home Meeting in Alabama during the time that Elwood C. Siler was Superintendent of the Yearly Meeting Evangelistic work.... She did not confine her service to the immediate family, many of the most precious years of her life being spent in active work in the field in the cause of temperance and social purity and as a minister of the Gospel in the truest sense. She gave freely of her time and means for the building of the schools and churches, traveling through the state soliciting funds.[5]

Sarah (Smith) [1802–1863] and Asaph Hiatt (Richland Friends, now known as Carmel Friends)

Both were ministers. He a slow, plain speaker. The ministry of both was that of exhortation.[6]

The Hiatts built a barn two miles south of Westfield which was used in the Underground Railroad. Sarah sat upon the WYM Committee for the Concern of the People of Color and the Committee to revise the *WYM Discipline*.[7]

Lydia (Kellum) [1798–1874] and Robert Tomlinson (Westfield/Chester Friends)

... were middle aged people; elders for many years, and active in the interests of the church. She, especially, was a leader. Conscientiously in their places at all services of the church, allowing no small matter or ordinary circumstance to interfere with this duty. Deeply interested in the Anti-Slavery movement and conscientious about using slave-labor goods. A journey to Greensboro, Indiana, was sometimes made, where free-labor goods could be obtained, Lydia refusing to purchase a calico dress when was known to have had in it the toil of a slave; and she preferred her coffee without sugar rather than use that coming from the cane-fields of the South. He was a conductor on the Underground Railroad, and their home was a refuge for many a poor, closely-pursued, runaway slave.[8]

CHAPTER SEVEN: DEACON, MINISTER, APOSTLE

Drusilla Wilson, c. 1870. First presiding clerk of Western Yearly Meeting for Business.

**Drusilla (1815–1906) and Jonathan Wilson
(Poplar Grove [Ridge] Friends)**

Drusilla moved to Hamilton County in 1851, and helped to begin Poplar Ridge Friends Meeting and Sabbath School (located in what is now Carmel, Indiana).

She and her husband were much interested in all church work in their early married life, and came to be useful and substantial members — pillars in the church — in middle and late life. They sympathized very much with the Anti-Slavery movement, but the visits, arguments and pleadings of some to induce them to join in the separation were met with a loving, "No friends, that is not the right way. Stay with the body of Friends and use our influence in that direction. . . ."

Her greatest campaign in reform work was for the prohibition amendment in Kansas. She and her husband traveled over three thousand miles in private conveyance during this warfare. She was the leading spirit in this great movement, holding at different times the office of State President, State Organizer, and State Treasurer of the Women's Christian Temperance Union.

The opening of our Yearly Meeting (Western) found Drusilla Wilson in the strength of her womanhood at the age of forty-three. She was chosen the first clerk of the WYM women's business meeting and served with wisdom and dignity for several years. [*A presiding clerk among Friends provided oversight for women's business meetings and created opportunities to train women in leadership. Today, Friends men and women meet together for business sessions.*] She was one of the first in WYM to encourage the organization of Scripture schools. She was ever aggressive, yet very careful not to get too far in advance of the body of the church. . . .[9]

Drusilla helped to establish a Mission Home for Girls (a forerunner to the Bertha Ballard Home) and was active in ministry until later in life when she made temperance addresses, conducted Bible studies, and later served as an elder of Indianapolis First Friends. She was recorded as a minister in 1885.

The legacy of recorded Friends women in ministry inspires me and is often unwritten for the twentieth century. Some yearly meetings no longer record Friends women in public ministry. Do you know the history of women in ministry leadership roles in your church?

Embracing an Endangered Testimony

The Friends meeting can be spiritually nurturing for those seeking to know the living Christ Jesus as Friend, and an encouraging place to faithfully grow and live out the fruits and gifts of the Holy Spirit, bestowed on those who deepen their relationship with Christ. Others in the Friends church often see our faithfulness to God's call before we are aware of it in our own lives.

As a teen in the Grinnell First Friends Church (Iowa Yearly Meeting), I was invited into membership, attended monthly meeting for business, and placed on a committee while I was still in high

CHAPTER SEVEN: DEACON, MINISTER, APOSTLE

school. I served as a youth group officer and taught Sunday School to preschoolers in the old church basement kitchen, a handy place for giving out snacks, with my high school friend, Linda. It was in this church that I first spoke a message out of open worship, and was recommended after years of spiritual growth and study to be recorded in ministry. The spiritual nurture of my faith and the encouragement of my first steps in ministry by the adults of the meeting made a big impact in my life.

Attending a Friends college also greatly influenced my life. As a student at William Penn College, I was encouraged to step up into new levels of ministry. Professor Edith Glover and Professor Willard Shaw, both members of the Friends Church, were faculty members teaching elementary education, which was my major. They provided me with a field education site at College Avenue Friends Church's Jack & Jill Preschool, working with Iola Cadwallader. She worked as the director for fifteen years and had developed an experiential "play-based" curriculum for the children. Iola was such an encouragement to me.

Iowa Yearly Meeting opened new avenues for a variety of ministries, as I counseled at Quaker Heights Camp, organized children/youth programming for yearly meeting sessions, and provided ministry with a Penn Christian Fellowship gospel team that traveled to Friends Churches on Sunday mornings. It was Iowa Yearly Meeting that recorded me as a minister of the Gospel of Jesus Christ, during the time when Steve and I were laboring spiritually together in Chicago, and thus opened up forty years and more of active ministry for me.

Too often the church today separates children and youth from the adults of the church to be a Sunday "audience." The rich sense of the church community is missing when we embrace worship as "parallel play." Youth are placed in peer groups which often suddenly evaporate after high school graduation. Relationships are not woven into spiritual friendships with the adults of the meetings, the spiritual gifts of the youth are not recognized and nurtured, and doors are not opened for meaningful service. Years later the church wonders what has happened to a generation who is not present.

With today's dramatic political and religious global changes affecting the lives of countless young girls and women, in many countries educational opportunities are still prohibited to them. Millions are denied the freedom to attend public worship, or even privately study the religious faith of their fathers. Just think of the advancement of women internationally if all branches of the Church Universal discerned and encouraged the developing spiritual faith and gifts of the girls and women in their midst. How might Friends once again historically lead the way in advancing the cause of faith-filled women by equipping and releasing them for vigorous public ministry and evangelism?

Think how the church might revive if women were encouraged to be faithful to a call to ministry today.

Are Friends today ready to commission women to radically preach the Good News of the risen Christ, as Jesus Himself did with Mary Magdalene?

CHAPTER EIGHT

Generosity
Mary of Bethany

A simple joy is a sunrise or a sunset. There is something about the emerging sun on the horizon at dawn as it pierces the darkness with bursts of color announcing a new day of life. Who doesn't love to hear the mother robin in an elm shade tree teaching her babies to sing on a springtime morning? I stop and ask God to lead me throughout the day. As twilight looms, with a thankful heart I marvel at the setting sun's beauty and the blessings of the day — God is good!

So much of our level of joy and gratitude is based on our ability to see God daily at work in our lives as blessings unfold, even in small things! A thankful heart — being "prayed up" with God — can change our life even in the midst of life's difficulties or times of sorrow.

The spiritual discipline of prayer develops an attitude of gratitude. Friends scholar and theologian Richard Foster shared the importance of prayer in his book, *Celebration of Discipline*.

> Prayer catapults us onto the frontier of the spiritual life. Of all the Spiritual Disciplines, prayer is the most central because it ushers us into perpetual communion with the Father. Meditation introduces us to the inner life, fasting is an accompanying means, study transforms our minds, but it is the Discipline of prayer that brings us into the deepest and highest work of the human spirit. Real prayer is life creating and life changing.[1]

To sit in the presence of Christ Jesus and to pray is to be open to responding with thanksgiving, compassion, and generosity of service. Through prayer, the "eyes of our hearts" are opened. A New Testament woman whose life was changed through listening to Jesus is Mary of Bethany.

Silent Meeting, by J. Walter West (1860–1933).

Mary of Bethany Listening at the Feet of Christ

Mary of Bethany's witness unfolds in three separate incidents found in the New Testament — a trilogy of a woman's life of prayer to 1) listen to the Word of Christ Jesus, 2) confess the need for Jesus in the midst of pain and suffering, and 3) generously minister for Christ Jesus out of gratitude.

Just prior to Mary of Bethany's story in the tenth chapter of Luke, a young lawyer comes not to listen to Jesus, but to test Him. The lawyer asks, "What must I do to inherit eternal life?" followed by the question, "Who is my neighbor?" These probing questions from the lawyer led Jesus to tell the Parable of the Good Samaritan. The hero of the story is not the priest or the Levite, but a Samaritan man who was considered unclean by many Jewish leaders of that day. The hero of the story is not the priest or the Levite, but a Samaritan man who was considered unclean by many Jewish leaders of that day. The Samaritan is the one who helps the wounded Jewish man who been a victim of crime.

Following this amazing parable about the importance of faith being put into action is Jesus' visit to the home of two sisters, Mary and Martha.

CHAPTER EIGHT: GENEROSITY

This real-life episode of two sisters demonstrates how our loving service of hospitality must never overshadow taking time to listen to Jesus Christ. Listening to Jesus is foundational!

> But the Lord answered her, 'Martha, Martha, you are worried and distracted by many things; there is need of only one thing. Mary has chosen the better part, which will not be taken away from her.
> — LUKE 10:41-42

If you have ever lived with sisters, Jesus' description of the dynamics between Mary and Martha feels so familiar. Martha "welcomed" Jesus and became busy focusing on the duties of hospitality. Instead of helping Martha, Mary chooses to sit at the feet of Jesus and listen. We often pass over the significance of this, since women were not allowed to be taught at the feet of a rabbi. However, Jesus allowed Mary to sit at His feet and to listen! Jesus does not rebuke Mary, but instead strives to edify Martha.

Both sisters are focused on "right" things. However, we need to sit ourselves down and spend time listening to Jesus, or we miss the part of infusing love in our service. It's not about us! If God's love isn't flowing into us, how can it flow out to others? Mary chose the better part and is found at the feet of Jesus listening.

Mary of Bethany Confesses Her Need

Mary again is found at the feet of Jesus in John 11:1-45.

Lazarus, the brother of Mary and Martha, had a serious illness. They sent for Jesus to come, but Jesus tarried and Lazarus died. As Jesus and the disciples approached Bethany, Martha went out to meet and confront Him. "Lord, if you had been here, my brother would not have died."

Jesus told Martha a precious truth, "I am the resurrection and the life. Those who believe in me, even though they die, will live, and everyone who lives and believes in me will never die." (John 11:25, 26a). Martha goes to Mary and says privately, "The Teacher is here and is calling for you."

Mary quickly went to Jesus and knelt weeping at His feet. She, too, wondered why her brother had to die. She thought Jesus loved them. Mary's heart was full of grief. If only Jesus had come!

We now see why it is important to have Jesus Christ as Friend. **We need to believe regardless of our circumstances!** Jesus loved this family and wept with them in their grief. Mary and Martha were not alone in their sorrow! Jesus, whose power was still at work, went to the tomb and raised Lazarus from the dead. Ironically, this supernatural gift of life to Lazarus led Jesus' enemies to plot His death.

Mary of Bethany's Generosity

In the next chapter of John, Jesus was invited to a dinner with Mary, Martha, and Lazarus (John 12:1-11). Lazarus sat with Jesus at the table while Martha again served. This family loved Jesus and no doubt were still reeling with amazement and gratitude for the miracle of Lazarus' resurrection.

For the third time, Mary of Bethany is found at the feet of Jesus. This time she is serving, too. Her service is not motivated by the demands of her sister Martha. Mary's service is an outpouring of generosity and love. Mary takes a pound of costly perfume made of pure nard, and anoints Jesus' feet, then wipes them with her hair, filling the air with the fragrance of the lavish gift. Her generosity of service now draws criticism from the disciple Judas, who thinks Mary should have sold her nard, then donated the money for the poor. But Mary's focus of service is on Jesus, who brought her brother back to life. No expense is too great or excessive. The outpouring of Mary's thankfulness is evident in her actions.

This trilogy of stories about Mary of Bethany stands in contrast to the Jewish lawyer who came to test Jesus about the requirements of Jewish law in Luke 10. He wanted to know the boundaries of love and service to justify his life. Mary of Bethany demonstrates a new understanding of service — someone whose life and friendship with Jesus Christ leads to overflowing generosity and service in His name. She sits at the feet of Jesus Christ, listens to His teachings, confesses her need for Him, and demonstrates her extravagant love and actions. Mary's changed life and her witness touched the lives of others.

Ministry of Service

Eliza Armstrong Cox

Once we embrace generosity of service, we often discover learning to serve with others is a powerful witness. This was the ministry of recorded Friends minister Eliza Armstrong Cox (1850-1935), a granddaughter of Asenath (Hunt) and Dougan Clark.

Eliza worked to gather women together to support Friends missionary efforts. In 1881, Eliza approached her friend, Jemima Pray, of the White Lick/ Mooresville Friends meeting (WYM), to begin a group for women focused upon missionary service. The first gathering was in the home of Rebecca J. Macy in March, 1881. Eliza wrote, "My heart leaped for joy."[2] Letters to Ella Davis (Vermilion Quarter), Mary Hadley (Bloomingdale Quarter), and Sarah King (Hamilton County) invited them to join these women the following September. They convened in Plainfield, Indiana, for the first meeting of what would become the United Society of Friends Women. Soon officers and a constitution were approved, and the way was opened now to "go forward." This ongoing organization of Friends women provided prayer and financial support for those called to missionary service for generations.

A recipient of this support was Mary Glenn Hadley (1939-2020), of Iowa Yearly Meeting. Mary Glenn's life demonstrated her faith in Christ Jesus, her loving service to His people at home and overseas, and her deep commitment to prayer and the Scriptures. Mary Glenn writes about her call from God to mission service:

Mary Glenn Hadley with student nurses in Kenya.

I grew up in a pastor's home where there was a positive concern for missions. Missionaries frequented our home when they were on furlough. Hearing missionaries speak was intriguing, but it was a classmate of mine, probably in second or third grade, who made me start thinking that maybe one day we could be missionaries. Was that a possibility?

It was a step of faith when I ventured to Iowa Methodist School of Nursing in Des Moines, Iowa, and did the necessary testing to see if I could be accepted into their school. I believed that if I was accepted that it was God opening the way. I started to nurses' training that fall and discovered that I loved what I was learning. Academically it was challenging. I lived and worked with people whose lifestyles and priorities were much different from mine. I realized my year at William Penn College had actually made me stronger in my faith and helped keep me from yielding to the temptations I found at the school of nursing.

It was my second year of training that God laid on my heart that I needed to contact mission boards to discover what educational requirements were required to be considered for service. Though I wrote letters to two mission boards, I carried them around quite a while before I found courage to mail them. The responses from both were very disappointing. I remember having a long conversation with God. I told Him that I had taken the step I felt led to do and now if this was a calling from Him, He would need to take the next step.

It was at church on a Sunday evening gathering, some time later, when the pastor and I were washing dishes after a shared meal. He asked me if I had ever considered missionary service. I remember hesitating to answer yet knowing in my heart that God was taking the next step. I told him that I did feel God was leading me to mission service and that I had made contacts with two mission boards but found their responses very disappointing. I did not know that he was actually on the FUM mission board but he told me that they were looking for a nurse to go to Kenya. Would I allow him to bring up my name?

The Friends United Meeting mission board contacted me fairly soon. When I met with them, I was taken back when the opening sentence of the conversation was, "We want you to know that you have been appointed to go to Kenya, East Africa, in September, 1962." God had to be direct with me so I would not doubt it was from Him. One verse of Scripture that spoke to me was John 15:16: "You did not choose me but I chose you. And I appointed you to go and bear fruit, fruit that will last, so that the Father will give you whatever you ask him in my name."

I wasn't quite twenty-three when I left for Kenya less than a year after graduating from nurses' training. There was so much to learn about living in a different culture with many different traditions. God led me through it all. Had He told me all the things that would be required of me at the beginning, I would never have been willing to go. However, He knew when to lead me to undertake tasks beyond my education or abilities because I was ready to go deeper in my relationship with Him. It often meant searching Scriptures, spending time in prayer to understand what He was saying to me but I became willing to accept the responsibilities and to trust Him to prepare the way, the people, the resources. I thank God today for the privilege He gave me to serve Him not only in Kenya but in the various ministries He has given me the opportunity to serve.

Mary Glenn helped to begin a ministry of prayer among the Kenyan Friends women and later became the President of the United Society of Friends Women International. This humble servant was faithful to listen in prayer and to generously serve Christ Jesus and His people in Kenya for over fifteen years.

Another faithful recorded Friends minister noted for his service was John Woolman (1720–1772). John had grown up within a Friends family, was educated at a Friends school, and attended Friends meeting, but as a teen he knew he was moving from the "flock of Christ" and found he was on a road associating with others "in that which is averse to true friendship." During this time, John "experienced the love of God, through Jesus Christ" in his life. He became acquainted with the language of the "true Shepherd" (John 10), and was recorded as a Friends minister at the age of twenty-three. John wrote about his call to true gospel ministry in his journal:

> Being thus humbled and disciplined under the cross, my understanding became more strengthened to distinguish the pure spirit which inwardly moves upon the heart, and which taught me to wait in silence sometimes many weeks together, until I felt that rise which prepares the creature to stand like a trumpet, through which the Lord speaks to his flock.
>
> From an inward purifying, and steadfast abiding under it springs a lively operative desire for the good of others. All the faithful are not called to the public ministry; but whoever are, are called to minister of that which they have tasted and handled spiritually. The outward modes of worship are various; but whenever any are true ministers of Jesus Christ, it is from the operation of His Spirit upon their hearts, first purifying them, and thus giving them a just sense of the conditions of others. This truth was early fixed in my mind, and I was taught to watch the pure openings, and to take heed lest, while I was standing to speak, my own will should get uppermost, and cause me to utter words from worldly wisdom, and depart from the channel of the true Gospel ministry.[3]

Through the power of the Holy Spirit's calling of John Woolman to travel in the ministry concerning the evils of slave holding, Philadelphia Yearly Meeting approved purging themselves from slavery in 1758.

CHAPTER EIGHT: GENEROSITY

The path of service to others is one often trod by those who feel called to public ministry. Our own lives must "speak" the message we feel called to "preach" in order for our ministry to be effective.

Witness of Service in our Daily Lives

Being the oldest of seven children, I was often called upon for service in the family. However, to this day I confess — I still do not like doing dishes. We lived in an old farm house with no dishwasher, so in our large family dish washing was often one of my tasks I had to be nagged to do.

One day my extended family came over to our home for a Sunday afternoon gathering. Normally this family met at the Iowa Lum Hollow family farm for a Weber family reunion around the Fourth of July weekend. For some reason, several of my grandmother's extended family had arrived at our home, and the women of the family were enjoying this rare opportunity to visit with each other. Without saying anything, I had started to tackle the stacks of dishes which were piling up in the kitchen. This was shortly after I attended Explo '72, a youth conference in Dallas, Texas, held at the Cotton Bowl, that drew over 80,000 high school and young adult people for six days of training in "personal evangelism, with a vision toward world evangelism, and to encourage attendees to seek some form of Christian service career."[4] During this experience my life had been touched by the Holy Spirit, for ministry. My spirit and thoughts still elevated from that signature event, I surprised myself by taking the initiative for doing THE DISHES!

My grandmother remarked, "What has come over Marlene? She is out doing the dishes for the family!" She noticed my act of loving service!

This chore I had previously detested had unconsciously become an act of joyful service to the women in my family who had given so much to me. I had not anticipated they would notice, but they did. I have to admit — I still don't like to do dishes. Nevertheless, I do believe the Holy Spirit does transform our lives into vessels through which His love flows to others.

The ministry of the Chicago Fellowship of Friends provided many opportunities for service throughout the years. One of the first occasions was in the renovation of our meetinghouse at 515 West Oak. Since it had been scheduled for demolition, for years it was an ongoing task of hosting almost-monthly work crews that helped to bring the building back from the brink of destruction. The women of the church played a primary role in making this corner building centrally located in Cabrini-Green a viable site for ministry. One of the first tasks was to feed the work crew volunteers who often originated from other Friends meetings. We renovated a room into a kitchen and began to serve meals on Saturdays to the volunteers. After lunch, we would set aside time to talk with the work crew members about the Cabrini-Green community and the vision for urban ministry. Fried chicken and/or catfish, cornbread, macaroni and cheese, greens, sweet potato pie, caramel cake, and banana pudding were some of my favorite menu items. The Chicago Fellowship of Friends women participated in the volunteer work by helping to scrape paint, plaster, and paint every wall. In the evenings, we often took everyone to eat stuffed pizza.

These work days were opportunities for service and hospitality. Through these volunteer work crews we revived the building for ministry, but also worked to build community within our own meeting and across Friends.

Prayer is a vital part of preparing our lives for generous loving service in ministry. Our work is to be motivated by the love of God through Jesus Christ, not our own ego. Discernment of the voice of the Good Shepherd calls us to ministry in His flock, the church of Jesus Christ.

What does the Good Shepherd say to you?

CHAPTER NINE

Hospitality and Spirit-Led Worship
Mary, Mother of Mark

Our home is our sanctuary. It is here with our family that we are best known. Our homes are not just filled with our loved ones and most treasured possessions, they are filled with memories of our lives' most precious moments. It is here that we seek sanctuary from the stress of life and solace for our souls. Our homes are also the center of our hospitality to others. It is here that people glimpse into the reality of our lives and we share with others what is most important to us. What do you cherish about your home?

One piece of furniture which has traveled with us through our transitions of pastoral homes is our kitchen table. This round butcher block pedestal table was one of our first purchases as a young married couple. There are personalized marks on the tabletop from years of our family life, often crumbs of food in the cracks, and one of the table's leaves is drooping from wear, but this piece of furniture is dear to my heart. I can picture myself, my husband, and my children around this table where we gathered for so many meals. Their place at the table will always be engrained in my memory.

Today this table is near the patio door of our kitchen and it is here that I sit for my morning devotions. Next to the table is an 1800s Morrison China Cabinet which has been passed down from my great-grandmother, and houses my Bible and journal I use each morning. As the morning light streams into the room, I can easily transition into the Lord's presence. It is where I shut out the cares of the world and center my heart for His "spiritual food" to nourish me for the day's events. It is where I listen for the Holy Spirit to speak — *a simple joy.*

Mary, Mother of Mark

The home also played a significant role in the New Testament Church. It was in an upper room that Jesus gathered with His disciples for the Last Supper (Mark 14:12-15). It was in this upper room where they gathered for prayer and were filled with the Holy Spirit (Acts 1:12-14; 2:1-14). In the New Testament, we are given one verse as to the identity of an amazing Jerusalem home where the early church gathered for prayer — it belonged to a woman named Mary!

> As soon as he [Peter] realized this, he went to the house of Mary, the mother of John whose other name was Mark, where many had gathered and were praying.
> — ACTS 12:12

It is this home of Mary, the mother of Mark, to which Peter fled when he was miraculously delivered from jail by an angel. Before this imprisonment, Peter was led by the Holy Spirit into new avenues of ministry. In Acts 10, the Holy Spirit had given him a vision three times — a special number for Peter indicating Jesus was speaking to him (three times he was found sleeping instead of praying in the Garden, three times he betrayed Jesus, three times he was asked to feed Jesus' sheep, and three times Peter saw a vision of unclean animals in a sheet). When the Roman Centurion Cornelius sent his three men to Peter, Peter went with them. "The Spirit told me to go with them and not to make a distinction between them and us" (Acts 11:12).

After this house call, which led to the conversion of a Roman centurion, Peter was imprisoned during the Jewish Passover in Jerusalem. No doubt the early church feared a repeat performance of the crucifixion of Jesus Christ! Also, James, the brother of John, had just been martyred. In these unsettling times, the church gathered for prayer in Mary's home.

As the church earnestly prayed, an angel appeared in Peter's prison cell and a "light shone in the cell." The angel awakened Peter, the chains fell from his wrists, and Peter followed the angel past the guards to freedom. Peter described to the church how the Lord rescued him from prison, and instructed them to make this report to Jesus' brother James, before Peter left from Mary's home.

Even though Mary's role is not highlighted in Acts, her ministry in the early church is to be noted. In this passage of scripture, we realize Mary is described as the mother of John Mark who wrote the Gospel of Mark.

Mark, the son of Mary, was a significant leader in the early Church and the author of the earliest written gospel in the New Testament. John Mark was born in what is now known as Cyrene, Libya — John was his Jewish name and Mark was his Roman name. After his birth, Mark's Jewish family migrated to Jerusalem. It is here that Mark became an eye witness to Jesus' life, and one of the seventy apostles. The Coptic church tradition tells us that Peter was married to Strapola, a relative of Mark's father. Barnabas, another prominent Christian disciple, was a brother of Mark's mother.[1] Considered the first pope of Alexandria (Egypt), Mark is seen as the father of African Christianity.

Mary's home of gathered prayer represents a shift in the understanding of worship by the New Testament church. As noted in the earlier discourse between Jesus and the Samaritan woman, location of true worship is not important. What is important to Jesus Christ is that God be worshipped in Spirit and in Truth (John 4:21-24). Thus, elaborate rituals in a temple by aristocratic religious authorities or exact adherence to outward religious law while one's heart remains untouched by God's Holy Spirit is not in unity with the new direction of the early church. The outpouring of the Holy Spirit was given freely to believers who gathered in prayer — even at the home of a woman named Mary.

Gathered Prayer

Early Friends often met for focused prayerful worship in homes or unassuming buildings. Where they gathered was called a "meetinghouse" since the "church" was the people, not the building. Their Protestant belief in the priesthood of believers extended to

Grace Church Street Meeting, c. 1880s. Artist unknown.

its logical conclusion — as the Holy Spirit fell upon the Church, men and women were empowered for ministry. Through belief in Jesus Christ, the Second Adam, we pass through the flaming sword and are restored into the relationship with God we were created to have — walking with God in holiness (Romans 5).[2] Through such convictions early Friends believed that Primitive Christianity could be restored.

As early Friends gathered for prayer in the name of Christ Jesus, they waited in silence. As promised in Matthew 18:20, they sensed the presence of the Living Christ in their midst and the covering of the Holy Spirit in the meetings for worship.

George Fox wrote of the importance of gathering for prayer in the Name of Christ Jesus in his pastoral epistles.

> You that are gathered in the Name of Jesus, whose Name is called the Power of God . . . for his Name's sake have you suffered all along. . . .
>
> His Name is a strong tower. So . . . You are in the strong tower, in which is safety and Peace . . . gathered in the Name of Christ Jesus,

> whose Name is above every name.... Above all other names and gatherings are you gathered... by which Salvation is given... and by this you come to fathom all other names under the whole heaven and to see... that there is no Salvation in them.... This is the standing gathering, in the Name, in the strong tower.... Rejoice you all that are brought into this gathering and have bowed to the name of Jesus.[3]

Gathered prayer in the name of Jesus Christ breaks down barrier walls among people who may not have known each other prior to meeting for worship. We become members of the "household of God" with Christ Jesus as the cornerstone of the church (Ephesians 2:13–22). Our Lord Christ Jesus is our peace. This is a deep peace which the world cannot give and can never understand.

Thomas Kelly, a twentieth-century Friends theologian, wrote of the reality of the "blessed community," the church.

> But every period of profound re-discovery of God's joyous immediacy is a period of emergence of this amazing group inter-knittedness of God-enthralled men and women who know one another *in Him*. It appeared in vivid form among the early Friends. ... The disclosure of God normally brings the disclosure of the Fellowship. We don't create it deliberately; we find it and we find ourselves increasingly within it as we find ourselves increasingly within Him. It is the holy matrix of the 'communion of the saints,' the body of Christ which is His Church.[4]

When we gather as the Church in the name of Jesus Christ, we are strengthened to do God's will. The New Testament church was ignited for ministry as described by another twentieth-century Friends theologian, D. Elton Trueblood:

> What we know is that it was the incendiary character of the early Christian fellowship which was amazing to the contemporary Romans and that it was amazing precisely because there was nothing in their experience that was remotely similar to it. Religion they had in vast quantities, but it was nothing like this. Consequently, the Romans, even the best of them, had no inkling of what was coming in the message of the early Church. Ceremonies they had galore, even Julius Caesar being a chief priest, but "Religion in the first century, B.C., had no stirring message of hope for the masses of Rome."

The metaphor of fire would be meaningless without the fellowship, because it has no significance for merely individual religion, as it has none for merely ceremonial religion. Though it is, of course, impossible to have a committed Church with uncommitted members; the major power never appears except in a shared experience. Much of the uniqueness of Christianity, in its original emergence, consisted of the fact that simple people could be amazingly powerful when they were members one of another. As everyone knows, it is almost impossible to create a fire with one log, even if it is a sound one, while several poor logs may make an excellent fire if they stay together as they burn. The miracle of the early Church was that of poor sticks making a grand conflagration. A good fire glories even its poorest fuel. . . .

Evangelism occurs when people are so enkindled by contact with the central fire of Christ that they, in turn, set others on fire.[5]

Worship is not meant to be a spectator sport.

The Presence of Christ in our Midst

My first childhood experience of gathered prayer came in the Friends Church of my childhood in Iowa. Each Sunday when we gathered for morning worship, there would be a period of silent, open worship. To sit in silence with a community of believers brings a holy hush. At first you seem drawn to listening to what is happening around you — the cry of a baby, the song of a bird outside the meetingroom, or the patter of rain against the window panes. Eventually you are drawn to the deep listening to the Living Christ within your heart. As a youth, I would bring my Bible to worship and would read Scripture which set my mind on God's Word.

In this gathering, Friend and octogenarian Orpha Taber Greene (my great-aunt's mother-in-law) always sat near the front of the meetingroom on a wooden pew marked with her well-worn seat cushion. On Sunday mornings, she would stand and lead us in vocal prayer out of the silence. For me it was a holy invocation of God's presence — inviting the covering of the Holy Spirit as we worshiped. I felt loved and welcomed into the presence of God. When I first

CHAPTER NINE: HOSPITALITY AND SPIRIT-LED WORSHIP

The Presence in the Midst, by James Doyle Penrose (1862–1932), (Matthew 18:20).

saw James Penrose's painting, *The Presence in the Midst*, I knew this is what I had been experiencing in gathered prayer — it was the presence of the Living Christ Jesus.

When I hear Christians talk about the importance of hospitality in the church today, they often refer to the staging of our building. What is our church's "curb appearance?" Do we have smiling greeters at the door? Is the meetinghouse clean and welcoming? Are we utilizing technology to reach our youth? Do we have publications which communicate our identity? Are coffee and refreshments offered? Although it is nice to think that our churches are willing to invest in our infrastructure, Christian hospitality is so much more than a veneer, no matter how well-polished.

The Chicago Fellowship of Friends had a powerful witness of hospitality that was more than an outward décor in the midst of a violent community where gang violence and the death of children from gunfire occurred too frequently. Our meeting room, located in our cinder block basement, had simple folding chairs, but more

Charlotte Thomas and student Condra working at the Young Friends after-school program.

important than anything outward was the Holy Spirit which covered our meetings for worship. A toxic congregation cannot gloss over the lack of genuine loving hospitality, nor can they gather people in the deep peace found in Christ Jesus.

When we first began to worship at the Chicago Fellowship of Friends on Oak Street, Steve would often sit on a folding chair on a summer Sunday morning in front of the meetinghouse doorway, greeting people as they passed our building, and letting them know all were welcome to come and worship. One day he greeted Charlotte, the sister of a young man Steve had met when he first came to Cabrini.

She told Steve that day, "I am looking for God."

"He's here, come on in," Steve encouraged.

As we sat in silent worship that morning, we could hear Charlotte quietly weeping, and she shared that she had met God!

CHAPTER NINE: HOSPITALITY AND SPIRIT-LED WORSHIP

She became a member of the Chicago Fellowship of Friends. Charlotte and her daughter helped on staff with the Young Friends after-school program. After graduating from college, Charlotte went on to get a full-time job in child care. Not only had she met God that day, but she met a community of faith which embraced her and walked with her in the Christian life. Charlotte had found a place where she could gather with others for prayer. Often during open worship, she would pray thanking the Lord for waking her up that morning — God is good!

One year I traveled to Mombasa, Kenya, for a United Society of Friends Women International conference. My sweet memories were not the elaborate trappings of what some United States churches consider hospitality. I remember being met by a stranger with a smile and a red rose. I remember fellowship over a cup of tea with new friends and times of spiritual reflection over meals. I remember heartfelt worship with inspired preaching by the Kenyan women, and our powerful times of prayer. Walls between strangers were broken down by the power of the Holy Spirit. I felt loved and welcomed! This genuine hospitality of the church is timeless!

True hospitality in the church invites people to sense the love of God and nurtures community. However, on Sunday mornings it is easy for our churches to become comfortable with familiar relationships, and begin to resemble exclusive clubs. Dr. Martin Luther King, Jr., at the end of a long interview on *Meet the Press* in April, 1960, declared, "I think it is one of the tragedies of our nation, one of the shameful tragedies, that 11 o'clock on Sunday morning is one of the most segregated hours, if not the most segregated hour, in Christian America."

Too often the church has slipped into political agendas and added to the division in churches and in our country. Community building and hospitality cannot be a mere token exterior effort. Gathered listening prayer in the name of Jesus Christ breaks down dividing walls and ignites the church — **a simple joy!**

Are you a spectator or gathered to glorify Christ Jesus?

CHAPTER TEN

Disciple
Tabitha/Dorcas

In the 1990s our country went through welfare reform. Cabrini-Green mothers were now required to search for work. Latchkey children in the Chicago Fellowship of Friends needed a new form of ministry which could meet their needs daily after school.

The old Jenner Elementary School was located on the north side of Oak Street in Chicago, and the Chicago Fellowship of Friends was located on the south side of Oak Street, just one-half block west of Jenner. This is the area that had been known as "Death Corner" during Prohibition. That spirit of violence continued for decades and even erupted in our time with the Fellowship of Friends. The Cabrini-Green gangs continued to fight to control the community's illegal drug trade, while the children dodged sniper bullets. It was in front of 500–502 West Oak, across the street from our meetinghouse, where a seven-year-old child, Dantrell Davis, was shot and killed by a Cabrini sniper as he walked to school with his mother. The Chicago Fellowship of Friends meetinghouse was at a significant and important location to provide a safe sanctuary for children after school in a community "at risk."

There was a need. . . . I had an elementary education degree . . . our meetinghouse was an old school building near a large urban elementary school in Chicago. The way opened for a new ministry, the Chicago Fellowship of Friends Young Friends After-School program.

Tabitha/Dorcas, Abounding with Deeds of Kindness

As the life of the early church unfolds in the book of Acts, we meet Tabitha, a woman who learned how to discern a need for ministry and respond. This New Testament woman's life abounded with deeds of kindness and she was given the title "Disciple" (Acts 9:36–42). A resident of Joppa, a Mediterranean coastal city that served as a primary seaport, Tabitha also had a Greek name, Dorcas.

Luke does not give us the words of Dorcas, but we are given an account of her abundant good deeds to the widows to whom she ministered and provided garments. We can understand why she would have been considered a disciple.

Then one day when Dorcas became ill and died, they sent for Peter. The weeping widows in the upper room where Dorcas lay gave witness to Peter of her good works for the poor. It was apparent that Dorcas had been active in ministry. Sending everyone from the room and kneeling, Peter simply prayed, "Tabitha, get up." A miracle occurred — Dorcas opened her eyes and sat up! Not only did she have a legacy of kindness and a roomful of ministry friends, but Dorcas' new life witnessed to many new believers in the Lord. Her life spoke!

In this passage, we witness Peter's practice of kneeling intercessory prayer to resurrect Dorcas. The early church knew they needed to send for Peter to pray. A humble attitude in kneeling prayer reflects it is not about us! It represents our dependence on God for a spiritual breakthrough.

Have you ever spent yourself in ministry to the point that you felt totally drained? Sometimes you give and give to the point you just stop. What a blessing to have someone who cares enough to come, kneel, and pray for you. Prayer works!

International Friends Women in Ministry

While at the Chicago Fellowship of Friends, the prayer support and acts of kindness shown to us by the United Society of Friends Women International (USFWI), which began through Eliza Armstrong Cox of Indiana, never ceased to amaze me. I felt surrounded by a multitude of praying witnesses whose encouragement empowered me for ministry (Hebrews 12:1–3).

When we began ministry at the Chicago Fellowship of Friends, these women pledged a portion of my salary. My witness of their abounding acts of kindness unfolded over the years: a John Sarrin Scholarship helped me attend seminary, greeting cards reminded me of their prayers, handmade quilts arrived to distribute to families in need, backpacks with school supplies came to us to give to children in our Young Friends After-School program, and shoeboxes of Christmas presents with hats and mittens were shared at our annual Christmas party. This kindness was further extended to me personally as I travelled in ministry to speak at a variety of Friends meetings. *These faithful Friends women prayed for me and I always sensed I was not alone in my travels and work.*

When I first experienced a meeting for worship with the Kenyan Friends women, I immediately felt at home. Their faith and prayer ministry melted away cultural and national walls and immediately gathered me into a sense of worship.

Mary Glenn Hadley shared how the anointed ministry of prayer impacted and reunited the Friends women of Kenya in her *United Society of Friends Women Kenya: Stories of Women with a Mission*:

> The Friends Church in Kenya was going through a lot of turmoil and strife in the 1970s which resulted in the formation of several yearly meetings. The USFW (United Society of Friends Women) found themselves caught in the middle of these divisions. In 1985, a group of women in the Kitale area started a prayer group which extended well beyond themselves.
>
> In 1989, nine women, representing each of the then four yearly meetings, flew to North Carolina to attend the USFWI Triennial. In a layover in LaGuardia Airport in New York, they began to ponder together over the dilemma in the Friends Church Kenya. One of the women said, "Isn't it time we did something about coming back together?" The group agreed but weren't sure how to proceed.
>
> God made the way known in 1991 when the USFW Kenya women were asked to provide a banquet for the FWCC (Friends World Committee for Consultation) world conference hosted at Chavakali. Women from then five yearly meetings worked together enthusiastically and served the banquet successfully. When the committee reviewed this accomplishment, one of the women made a suggestion wondering if the women could possibly continue to meet occasionally and pray together.

CHAPTER TEN: DISCIPLE

United Society of Friends Women International singing in Kenya, July 2010.

Three women had earlier had a conversation with the Women Coordinator of NCCK (National Council of Churches in Kenya), sharing their desire to pull together Friends women in unity. This Coordinator provided the next step when she told them she had found a donor to pay the cost for a workshop. The workshop was held in a neutral location, Nyeri Central Province. Women came from each of the five yearly meetings and experienced a lot of healing during this time.

In 1991, the women began to organize themselves as USFW-Kenya, meaning that the USFW groups from each yearly meeting would become a part of the larger USFW-Kenya group. There were three stated purposes for this group: 1) lead prayer gatherings, 2) visit all yearly meetings in order to reach as many people as possible, and 3) call for unity and love. Women responded well to meeting in prayer gatherings, some with great trust and others more cautiously. These gatherings were held every three months, meeting at first at Chavakali, but later meeting at different yearly meeting sites. These important prayer sessions helped to re-group and unite Friends women in Kenya.

Early on the women would gather for prayer and enjoy fellowship with tea. As the numbers increased to multiple thousands of women, it was not possible to provide the tea. Women would travel on the bus overnight to get to the prayer gathering and return home overnight following the prayer time. There is a strong sense of unity and purpose as they continue meeting for prayer and work together on common projects. They meet every three years as the USFW-Kenya Triennial. Prayer united these Friends women in Kenya who have made a remarkable impact on their yearly meetings.

Through discerning prayer, the way forward for ministry becomes clear.

Ministry of Kind Deeds

When we started the Chicago Fellowship of Friends Young Friends After-School program, we tried to simply provide a healthy snack after school and a safe place for the children until their mothers returned from work — safe school-aged child care. Soon I realized that most of our children had homework that needed to be completed and many of them also needed tutoring to complete their homework. Nearby Moody Bible Institute's Practical Christian Ministries Department students volunteered to help with these tasks. The academic performance of the children soon improved.

After homework was completed, we offered free and supervised play — a 4-H club, Girl Scouts, group games, and table games. We drove the children for free play in our vans to the amazing Oz Park Playground in the Lincoln Park community north of Cabrini-Green! Soon we were a part of the State of Illinois' Teen REACH program where we added life skills training. Block grant funds from a tobacco law suit provided monies to states to support life skills programs for "at risk" children and youth.

These programs helped youth to abstain from substance abuse, and also provided violence prevention training. We hired teens from our youth programs whose leadership provided an amazing role model for the Cabrini children. Later we added dinner provided by the Kids' Cafe of the Greater Chicago Food Depository. When the moms picked up their kids after work, their children had worked on or completed their homework, played safely with friends, and eaten dinner. Young Friends offered a positive peer group for children, a safe haven.

On Thursday nights the children were invited to stay late for our church's outreach ministry where we played games, sang songs, listened to a Bible story, and created an arts and crafts project. In our holistic ministry to the children, we could not neglect the spiritual component. One night after our youth club, when we had talked about being a peacemaker for Jesus Christ, a child came forward and gave me bullets he had been holding as a "shortie," a child new to a gang. Who says we do not need to preach the Good News of the gospel today? Peacemaking is needed in our cities!

During the summers we expanded our program to full days. Each week we would plan amazing outings throughout the Chicago area: the DuSable Museum of African American History, the Lincoln Park Zoo, the Chicago Botanic Gardens, the Chicago Children's Museum, swimming at Moody Bible Institute, the Shedd Aquarium, the Field Museum of Natural History, the Adler Planetarium, the Museum of Science and Industry, roller skating, ice skating, and the theater. Often the prices were reduced or our fees waived. Each month we would go out to eat at a local restaurant to celebrate the birthdays of the children. We would even take the kids to a week of Quaker Haven Camp in Syracuse, Indiana, or visit farm families in Iowa and Indiana. The United Society of Friends Women donated books for our Young Friends After-School library and we developed a reading program with the local public library in Chicago's Near North Community. Grant money paid for our new after-school program computers. We expanded the experience of the children beyond the Cabrini-Green community. We could all see the students growing in self-confidence as their academic and social skills developed.

We had a group of amazing Cabrini-Green mothers and we were in it together for the kids! Whenever I return to Chicago, I love to visit these families because a deep bond of community occurred with these women and their children. I know what the disciple

Tabitha, and the women of Joppa who called upon Peter to save Tabitha's life, must have felt for each other.

Today our churches too often become cloistered from ministry needs. We enjoy hearing speakers who make us aware of current social concerns. We are willing to donate financial resources with a touch of our cell phones, and occasionally we may volunteer for special events or we work to have our special concern included in the church budget. What is missing is a most profound witness of Christianity — development of relationships and Christian community with those in need. We miss the mark if we are only trying to build up our reputation or resume by volunteering for Christian service!

The need for us to move beyond token service to discipleship as a way of life is also found in the words of Jesus Christ as He neared the end of His life:

> Then the king will say to those at his right hand,
> 'Come, you who are blessed by my Father,
> Inherit the kingdom prepared for you
> from the foundation of the world;
> For I was hungry and you gave me food,
> I was thirsty and you gave me something to drink,
> I was a stranger and you welcomed me,
> I was naked and you gave me clothing,
> I was sick and you took care of me,
> I was in prison and you visited me'. . . .
> And the king will answer them, 'Truly I tell you,
> Just as you did it to one of the least of these
> who are members of my family, you did it to me.'
> — MATTHEW 25:34–36; 40

What would Jesus Christ say to you and your church?

CHAPTER ELEVEN

Prayer and Praise
Lydia and the Women of Philippi

My husband Steve used to invite the Cabrini-Green pastors to our church on a monthly basis for donuts, coffee, worship, and prayer. This meeting developed relationships across the denominational boundaries: Friends, Baptists, African Methodist Episcopal, Presbyterians, Catholics, United Methodists, Church of God in Christ, and Non-denominational. A chance to talk about community needs and church activities occurred. The Near North Ministry Alliance was organized.

One day a young man was shot across the street from the Chicago Fellowship of Friends. Steve organized a press conference at our church. The silent churches of Cabrini-Green suddenly had a voice on the evening news as the ministers called for peace and

Cabrini-Green high-rise apartments, 1159-61 N. Larrabee, Chicago, IL.

a stop to violence. When the City of Chicago threatened to close the neighborhood elementary school due to the bloodshed, the ministers met with the Chicago Superintendent of Schools to fund their peace plan rather than close the school.

Cabrini-Green churches were given exterior signs to indicate safe sanctuary from gang violence. Trained parents were given cell phones and stationed on routes children walked to school to provide safety on the "hot spots" of violence. Additional after-school programs were developed for children and job training for parents. The churches began to work together in the midst of suffering to seek peace. Prayer and faithful ministry can transform suffering to become a powerful Christian witness for which we can praise God!

The Women of Philippi

After the death and resurrection of Jesus Christ and the persecution of the early church, Christians spread the message of the risen Lord into new areas. The leadership of women is seen in the subsequent growth of the New Testament church.

> The Lord opened [Lydia's] heart to listen eagerly to what was said by Paul. When she and her household were baptized, she urged us, saying, 'If you have judged me to be faithful to the Lord, come and stay at my home.' And she prevailed upon us.
> — ACTS 16:14b-15

In Acts 16, the Apostle Paul visited the Roman city of Philippi. Unlike Paul's practice to first preach at a Jewish synagogue, Paul and Silas went outside the city gate to a river where women gathered for prayer. Paul sat and spoke to the group which included a woman named Lydia, a dealer in purple cloth from the City of Thyatira and a "worshipper of God," perhaps a Gentile who never became officially Jewish.

This glimpse into urban evangelism reveals the important role women played. Obviously, Lydia was a woman of financial means and her hospitality to Paul and Silas helped to launch the Philippian church. Her convincing invitation to Paul is summarized by Luke, "and she prevailed upon us." Her leadership is seen and noted.

Luke now introduces us to another young woman of Philippi, a nameless slave girl whose owners made money from her fortune-telling abilities. Philippi was known as a location of the Delphic oracle whose symbol was a python. This powerful spirit supposedly spoke through people; the term "ventriloquist" described this ability.

As Paul and Silas passed by the slave girl on their way to the place of prayer, she called out, "These men are slaves of the Most High God, who proclaim to you a way of salvation" (Acts 16:17b). Realizing that deliverance was needed, Paul commanded the spirit, "I order you in the name of Jesus Christ to come out of her" (Acts 16:18b). At that very moment the slave girl was delivered by the name of Jesus Christ!

By setting this slave girl free, Paul and Silas lost their own freedom. They were brought before the local magistrates with the slave owners' complaints. These men of the Lord were stripped, severely beaten, and thrown into prison. Placed in an inner cell, they were fastened in stocks. After this ordeal, who could sleep?

At midnight Paul and Silas prayed. Singing hymns of praise to God, they gave a witness to everyone in the jail! Suddenly an earthquake shook the prison's foundation — chains fell from the prisoners and the jail door flew open. Fearing the terrible consequences of allowing prisoners to escape, the jailer drew his sword in order to take his own life.

Paul cried out, "Do not harm yourself, for we are all here." By his cries, Paul stopped the jailer's suicide, and then shared the Word of the Lord with him. Afterwards, the grateful jailer took Paul and Silas home, washed their wounds, and fed them. This family's testimony is another part of the emerging Philippian church, as Paul's efforts resulted in the baptism of the jailer's entire household, who all became believers in Jesus Christ. When Paul and Silas left the prison, they headed for Lydia's home where they were met by "the brothers and sisters" of the newly-forming faith community.

The New Testament includes Philippians, a short epistle written by Paul to the church started by Lydia and the women who

> *I thank my God every time I remember you, constantly praying with joy in every one of my prayers for all of you....*
>
> *And this is my prayer, that your love may overflow more and more with knowledge and full insight to help you to determine what is best, so that in the day of Christ you may be pure and blameless, having produced the harvest of righteousness that comes through Jesus Christ for the glory and praise of God.*
>
> — PHILIPPIANS 1:3-4, 9-10

gathered at the river to pray. Paul encouraged the Philippians to witness true joy in the midst of suffering. Considered the epistle of "joy," the concept of joy or rejoicing occurs sixteen times in this book. "Rejoice in the Lord always, I will say it again: Rejoice" (Philippians 4:4). Joy is one of the hallmarks of the Christian life and a powerful witness of overflowing love in the midst of the suffering experienced by these believers!

Bearing the Cross of Christ Jesus

The early Friends understood what it meant to walk faithfully in the light of Christ Jesus in what George Fox called a "crooked and perverse generation" (Philippians 2:15), even if it meant suffering. This belief was shared by another early convinced Friend, William Penn. At the age of twenty-two, Penn heard a powerful message by Quaker missionary Thomas Loe:

> (Thomas Loe) began his declaration with these words, 'There is a faith that overcomes the world and there is a faith that is overcome by the world' upon which subject he enlarged with much clearness and energy. By the living and powerful testimony of this man, which had made some impression on his spirit ten years before, he was thoroughly and effectively convinced and afterwards constantly attended the meetings of that people.[1]

Two years later Penn was inspired by Loe's dying words.

> 'Dear heart, bear thy cross, stand faithful for God and bear thy testimony in thy day and generation: and God will give thee an

eternal crown of glory, that none shall ever take from thee. There is not another way. Bear thy cross. Stand faithful for God. This is the way the holy men of old walked in and it shall prosper.[2]

These words inspired Penn while writing his spiritual classic *No Cross, No Crown* during the two years he was imprisoned in the Tower of London for his faith. The Friends knew how to nonviolently witness for their faith in the midst of suffering.

Most early Puritans did not allow women to preach. Fox wrote in his *Journal* of an encounter with those who declared women had no souls, "No more than a goose." George countered with the Scripture in which Mary said, "My soul doth magnify the Lord, and my spirit hath rejoiced in God my Savior."[3] Recorded Friends women ministers were fully recognized and released by the Religious Society of Friends both in England and in the colonies (and later the United States) to use their spiritual gifts as the Holy Spirit led. However, when preaching they often met with persecution from outraged community leaders and clergy.

An early Friends woman preacher who witnessed for her faith, resulting in severe punishment, was Mary Fisher. Born in 1624, Mary Fisher was a maid servant to Richard Tomlinson and his wife in Selby, of northern England. When Mary heard George Fox preach, she became a convinced Friend and began preaching with Mistress Tomlinson in Selby. Soon Mary was imprisoned at York Castle Dungeon for preaching her Friends message. During sixteen months of imprisonment, Mary met two other Friends women ministers, Elizabeth Hooton and Jane Holmes, who taught Mary how to read and write. Both Mary and Elizabeth, along with nine other women, eventually banded together with forty-nine male Friends primarily from northwest England, the "Galilee of Quakerism." Called the "Valient Sixty," these Friends ministers and missionaries traveled across Britain, then Europe and the American colonies, preaching their religious convictions, often in the face of bitter persecution.

Mary Fisher and Elizabeth Williams preached at Sydney Sussex College, a seminary in Cambridge where Oliver Cromwell was an early student. The women announced to the young theologians

Mary Fisher Before the Sultan of the Ottoman Empire, 1658, American wood engraving, artist unknown.

that their college was a "Cage of Unclean Birds."[4] The Mayor of Cambridge had the two Friends women ministers stripped naked to the waist and pinned to a post, where a violent whipping tore their flesh, leaving scars. Mary and Elizabeth "became the first Quakers to be publicly and brutally flogged for their ministry."[5]

Mary Fisher and Ann Austin felt called to take the Friends message to the Puritans of the Massachusetts Bay Colony. In 1656, they were the first Friends to arrive in Massachusetts. Their books and literature were seized and burned. Mary and Ann were imprisoned without trial, stripped, and searched for a sign of the devil on their bodies. After imprisonment, they were returned to England.

Perhaps Mary's most well-known journey in ministry was her visit to the Sultan Mehmed IV, who ruled the Ottoman Empire from 1648 to 1687. Despite concerns of violence, Mary brought her message from the Lord to the Sultan. When asked what Mary thought of Mohammed she said: ". . . she knew him not; but Christ, the true prophet, the Son of God, who was the light of the world, and enlightened every man coming into the world, Him she knew."[6] Mary returned to England safely from her obedient journey.

Obedience to Christ Jesus regardless of suffering is difficult. Christian women in the United States today are usually not jailed for their beliefs, but in other countries Christian women proclaiming the gospel are sometimes harshly punished and even executed. However, American Christian women are often sidelined or "cancelled" from endorsed or financially-supported ministries in the decision-making of their respective churches. As women, we are often told to be "silent" and listen. Too often we rationalize being silent as the "loving response," not wanting to rudely offend the "feelings" of those who disagree with us. When women are bullied by leaders in power who disagree with the voice of women, it is easy for lies and deception to occur. However, the Lord calls us to be faithful to His ministry, a ministry of Spirit and Truth that can convict, admonish, and at times offend. At those times we stand in the Light of Christ and fill our hearts with praise, as the Philippian Church learned.

The Power of Praise

Early in ministry I realized the power of prayer and praise in the midst of suffering. When it had been a rough day, I would remind myself of all the times the Lord had brought me through difficulties. Through prayer I reminded myself to remain faithful to carry the cross of Christ, no matter the "deep baptism" I experienced. I often read and prayed passages of Scripture to fill my heart with words of praise from God's Word.

Some of my "go to" Scriptures when I am troubled are from the book of Philippians. If we have the Word of God hidden in our heart, it helps us to stand in the midst of suffering and sorrow. The Philippian church testimony is a strong reminder that the Lord can gather us from humble beginnings, rescue us from evil, and fill our hearts with praise in suffering.

Singing praise to God in the midst of suffering breaks the chains that bind us in our life and is a powerful witness. Songs of praise in times of trials can encourage and heal when we have no words, and return our focus upon Christ Jesus. At our Young Friends After-School program, we organized a youth choir led by one of our high school staff members who had grown up through Young Friends. The children knew she lived on Oak Street in the Cabrini row houses and she was respected in the community for her faith. She was a great leader.

This youth choir had the opportunity to travel and sing at Friends churches. As we traveled, they stayed in the homes of Friends who were members of these churches. One of the choir's favorite songs at that time was "Stomp," by Kirk Franklin. I can still visualize these young people smiling, clapping, rocking, and singing joyously. Don't let me forget their "stomp!" Praise music restores and energizes my soul. Praise music is even more dynamic when we are gathered with others. It is a powerful witness to our faith.

The church has a powerful testimony of the importance of music in worship. When Jesus and his disciples had finished their last meal before His crucifixion and resurrection, they sang a hymn, then went out to the Mount of Olives (Matthew 26:30). George Fox could be heard singing hymns during the night hours while in his prison cell.

In addition to marvelous hymns and current praise music, some of my favorite songs are historic spirituals. If you are looking for music which communicates spiritual strength in suffering, who can forget such songs as "Hold On!" We need to cherish and continue to sing and teach the rich lyrics and deep poetry of the Church's songbook, old and new, which has a precious spiritual strength and communicates a deep spiritual truth.

In the midst of suffering, singing our theology centers us. I will never forget the power of hearing the Kenyan Friends singing, a cappella, the precious hymn "It Is Well With My Soul," when we gathered for worship. When things get us down, we need to turn our lives around with the love of Jesus. To gain the victory over troubles and sorrows, singing helps our spirits soar! Have we memorized songs that will fix our hearts and minds on Jesus Christ and the power and promises of Holy Scripture? What is our playlist of songs that lifts our hearts and spirits? Music gathers the church in the midst of suffering!

Prayerful obedience to Christ Jesus in the midst of suffering is a powerful witness seen in the early church of Philippi, in the lives of early Friends who suffered persecution for their faith, and in the oppressed church today. Singing hymns and songs of praise puts joy back in our hearts. It empowers us to take our eyes off our problems and to fasten them upon Christ Jesus. It is a strong witness of the abiding love, peace, and joy that the world cannot give.

The legacy and power of praise music can be heard in the ecstatic beauty of Beethoven's Ninth Symphony. American poet Henry van Dyke set the text of his "Hymn of Joy" to Beethoven's glorious music in 1907.[7] It is considered one of the greatest expressions of exhilaration and exultation in the English language. As van Dyke wrote,

> Joyful, joyful, we adore Thee
> God of glory, Lord of love
> Hearts unfold like flow'rs before Thee
> Op'ning to the Sun above
> Melt the clouds of sin and sadness
> drive the dark of doubt away
> Giver of immortal gladness
> fill us with the light of day
>
> Thou art giving and forgiving
> ever blessing, ever blest
> well-spring of the joy of living
> ocean-depth of happy rest
> Thou the Father, Christ our Brother —
> all who live in love are Thine
> Teach us how to love each other
> lift us to the Joy Divine

Do you have a favorite hymn or praise song that lightens your spirit and gives your heart joy?

CHAPTER TWELVE

Church Planter and Elder
Priscilla

One Sunday morning we were driving to a rural Indiana Friends Church to share during morning worship. We thought we had allotted enough time to reach our destination. Nevertheless, we had not anticipated summer road construction. Although a detour sent us out of our way to reach the church, it prevented us from entering a road where a bridge was under construction — a disaster waiting to happen.

Many of us have produced detailed life goals and have created a timeline to reach them. We may have even created detailed goals for our church and ministry. However, our lives can suddenly face disruption. Do we heed the warnings in life that can be annoying, but are often lifesaving: the health tests which disclose the advent of a disease which can be cured or more helpfully managed, the tornado sirens which signal the need to take cover when we are in the path of the storm, or lighthouses which send out a beam warning of rocky coastal shorelines?

Do we have people in our lives who provide spiritual warnings for us — who will speak the truth in love to us? Do we have a spiritual team to help us grow in discernment and spiritual maturity?

Priscilla and Aquila

This couple worked on Paul's ministry team to gather urban churches in the Roman Empire: Corinth, Ephesus, and Rome. In Acts 18:1-4, we learn that Paul met Priscilla and Aquila when he arrived in the city of Corinth. The couple had left Rome at the time Emperor Claudius banished "all Jews." Roman historian Suetonius pointed to a conflict recorded in Rome over "Chrestus," supposedly

CHAPTER TWELVE: CHURCH PLANTER AND ELDER

Christ, around this time. Corinth was the first church plant of this ministry trio.

At this time, Corinth was a major cosmopolitan city-state with a diverse population along with the site of the Temple of Aphrodite (Venus), the goddess of love, located on the summit of Acrocorinth. The multiple challenges in the Corinthian church plant can be uncovered in 1 and 2 Corinthians. In addition to Paul's challenge to the new believers, we find in 1 Corinthians (13:4–7, 13) his popular description of *agape* love, foundational for Christians. No doubt the women of Corinth understood the drastic contrast between the worship of Aphrodite in Corinth (*Greek eros* love) and the gospel message taught by the ministry team (*Greek agape* love).

> *Love is patient; love is kind; love is not envious or boastful or arrogant or rude. It does not insist on its own way; it is not irritable or resentful; it does not rejoice in wrongdoing, but rejoices in the truth. It bears all things, believes all things, hopes all things, endures all things. Love never ends . . .*
>
> *And now faith, hope, and love abide, these three; and the greatest of these is love.*
>
> —1 CORINTHIANS 13:4–8a, 13

The next church Priscilla and Aquila helped to establish was in Ephesus, the site of the Temple of Artemis, also known as the Temple of Diana, one of the Seven Wonders of the Ancient World. Artemis was considered a mother goddess who promised to give women assistance in fertility and child birth. This city was a great location to offer a Christian alternative to the worship of Artemis.

At Ephesus, we see the emerging pastoral leadership of Priscilla and Aquila as church planters with a church in their home (1 Corinthians 16:19). After their arrival in Ephesus, Paul departs (Acts 18), leaving Priscilla and Aquila to confront a challenge that must be addressed. It was apparent to them by his preaching that Apollos, "an eloquent man, well versed in the scriptures," who had arrived from Alexandria (Egypt), knew of the water baptism of John. Their concern was that Apollos' message was incomplete. In an attempt to better inform or "elder" Apollos, Priscilla and Aquila "explained the Way of God to him more accurately" (Acts 18:26b). They spoke "the truth in love" (Ephesians 4:15) concerning Apollos' message and the identity of Jesus as the Messiah. Their leadership helped Apollos and prepared him for future ministry in Achaia. Acts 18 states that Apollos, upon his arrival, greatly helped those who through grace had become believers, for he powerfully refuted the Jews in public, showing by the scriptures that the Messiah is Jesus (Acts 18:27b-28).

Our final glimpse of Priscilla and Aquila is their return to Rome where a church met in their home (Romans 16:3-4). Rome was the epicenter of the Roman Empire, where a form of state religion recognized Caesar not only as head of the state, but as divine. However, the early Christians did not believe Jesus Christ was merely another deity to be added to the pantheon of Roman gods. Conflict continued to escalate as Christians refused the syncretism of the Roman Empire. At the conclusion of the book of Romans (Paul's epistle), Priscilla and Aquila are recognized as "fellow workers in Christ Jesus." Their ministry legacy is apparent!

Helen and Jefferson Ford

One of the significant couples in the Friends missionary movement were Helen and Jefferson Ford, who helped to plant Friends churches in Western Kenya in the early twentieth century. Not only were the Fords evangelists, but the account of their ministry in the book, *The Steps of a Good Man*, provides an insight into Ford's call to ministry and the historic practice of "eldering" by Friends. Among Friends, elder was more than a noun — it was also a verb.

One Sunday morning in 1898, at the Cedar Avenue Friends Church where Jefferson was a member, he felt the Lord's call to ministry as he sat in worship.

> The windows were open, as it was a hot, sunny day. His [Jefferson's] spirit was communing with his Lord when he became conscious of a delicate fragrance and a soft breeze. He looked out the window. Not a leaf was stirring. He looked about him in wonder. Then, so

CHAPTER TWELVE: CHURCH PLANTER AND ELDER

Helen and Jefferson W. Ford and family, 1911. Photograph from *The Steps of a Good Man*. Photographer unknown.

> distinct was the voice of the Holy Spirit within his heart, it seemed audible to him. **'I have anointed thee to preach the Gospel.'** So wonderfully precious was that hour he rarely mentioned it. When he did, something of the awe and sacredness of that moment always crept into his voice.[1]

Soon thereafter, Jefferson graduated from Cleveland Bible Institute, where he had met a young woman named Helen Farr who eventually became his wife. Her family, Friends from Iowa Yearly Meeting, had served on the mission field in Jamaica. Jefferson and Helen's true call from God upon their hearts was to work in Kenya. They prayed for an open door and eventually moved to Westfield, Indiana. In 1913, they were told by the Mission Board of Five Years Meeting (later known as Friends United Meeting), ". . . to raise a stated amount for their support for five years, and secure pledges for travel **to and from** the field! Jefferson felt cast down in spirit by the conditions. He had never **asked** for a cent of money, and couldn't feel free to do so."[2]

Shortly after this, a farmer from the Friends Quarterly Meeting in Hamilton County, Indiana (Western Yearly Meeting), pledged a financial gift each month for the next five years. Soon the whole amount was pledged by local Friends. "It was a gracious seal of God's approval upon their going out, especially when it is remembered that there was a financial recession in America that year. This was the beginning of a series of miracles the whole journey through."[3] While the world prepared for World War I, Hamilton County Friends sent a missionary family to Kenya!

In 1914, the Fords left all that was dear and familiar to start their work in Lugulu, western Kenya. In her book, *The Steps of a Good Man*, the Fords' daughter Helen Kersey Ford writes of Jefferson recalling an "eldering" incident which helped spark a revival in Kenya.

> Tuesday at Mbale, a church near a large market, the power of the Spirit was felt in the first service. Afterwards a leading elder, Paulo Agoi, told Bwana he had no peace of heart because of a quarrel between his wife and his brother Samuel's wife, in which the husbands were involved. It had started over Paulo's chicken which had been eaten by the sister-in-law when it scattered her grain. The fight had spread to the whole village. Jefferson suggested that all four meet and try to clear up the trouble.
>
> When they came, one woman started complaining about the other. While silently praying, Jefferson gave each one her own chance. Now he suggested that each one confess her own wrong doing. Silence. Then Paulo confessed wherein he now saw he was wrong. Samuel followed, then the women. After asking each other's forgiveness, they all knelt and brokenly asked God's pardon for disrupting the whole village. When they arose with peace and joy, there were four pools of tears on the floor. This reconciliation cleared the way for the Lord to begin revival.
>
> Each day other missionaries came to join in. Many Christians confessed sins, sought forgiveness, and made peace with factions. Jefferson continued the preaching the third day with marked victories. He thought to begin a praise service which again turned into a time of confession. At the close of the session, seekers were invited to the school building. Surprisingly, that building

quickly filled with nearly 300 people. The meeting was opened for the expression of personal needs. One after another earnestly confessed failure before God. Some publicly asked pardon of others. As twilight crept in there was quiet weeping. The missionaries explained that since the Holy Spirit was at work, He could hear the petition of each, so they might all kneel and pray softly at the same time.

From burdened hearts, they sought forgiveness with tears such as the missionaries had rarely seen in Africa. Some rose to seek forgiveness for a wrong done. Faces were full of light and joy as they finally broke up to scatter to their homes.[4]

Ford worked with Joseph Litu and finished the translation of the Bible from English into Ragoli* that was first started by Emory Reese, and later published by the American Bible Society. He also founded what is now known as Friends Theological College. Today a brick church still stands in Lugulu that was built during the years when Jefferson and Helen Ford were in Kenya. Because of their devotion to the Lord and their faithful witness to the people of Kenya, many churches were planted and strengthened through the Ford's ministry.

Will the Real Elders Please Stand Up!

Discerning elders were vital among historic Friends. Elders and recorded ministers sat at the front of the meetinghouse to provide oversight over the meeting for worship. Friends elders and recorded ministers, in a spirit of worship, actively helped gather meetings to discern important decisions, what Friends call the "sense of the meeting." Elders were agents of "gospel order" for the church, a historic Friends testimony of peacemaking taken from Matthew 18:15-35. As shepherds of the church, they helped to discern the voice of Christ (Acts 20:17-38). Friends elders labored in love for Truth to be "lifted up."

---

*also known as Lugooli, one of the languages of the Luhya people.

Grinnell Friends Church, Grinnell, Iowa, Iowa Yearly Meeting — my home church.

The work of elders has been important in my life. In 1979, when I was in the recording process of Iowa Yearly Meeting and had completed all the requirements, the Training and Recording Committee prepared to bring my name forward for approval during yearly meeting annual business sessions. One pastor on the Committee suddenly disapproved of my recording, since he felt every other woman who was a pastor's wife would think they, too, should be recorded.

Upon hearing this news, my home monthly meeting, which had put my name forward for the recording process, wrote an additional minute to the yearly meeting affirming their approval of my becoming a recorded minister. During Iowa Yearly Meeting sessions, individuals from my home meeting, Grinnell Friends Church, and across the yearly meeting who had known me, stood on the floor during the discernment for the recording of ministers, to voice their support that I be approved as a recorded Friends minister.. I was recorded as "a minister of the Gospel with Full Rights and Privileges of Ministerial Status in the Friends Church." The voices of recorded ministers and elders from the yearly meeting helped the large gathering's approval of the "sense of the meeting" for me to become a recorded Friends minister. It was after this that I became a student at McCormick Theological Seminary in Chicago.

Later when we were in a ministerial position, the support of other Friends ministers and elders helped to renew our employment. As our contract was considered on the floor of the Administrative Council, a woman I had never seen before in a business meeting stood to say Steve and I were racist! Anyone who really knew us would have immediately recognized this false allegation since we had spent nearly thirty years of our lives involved in ministry in the Cabrini-Green public housing development. Two African American men who had been active Chicago Fellowship of Friends members, Willie Moore and Charlie Anderson, were present at this Western Yearly Meeting business meeting at Ridge Farm Friends Church. Surprised to hear the allegation, it was confronted and truth was spoken by them. Friends at the business session were told, "You don't know who you've got!" Willie had been an elder at the Chicago Fellowship of Friends and was at that time a representative of 57th Street Friends in Chicago. Our contract for the following two years was approved. I was so proud they were willing to speak the truth. This precious testimony of truth telling by recorded ministers and elders is vital among Friends.

Friends elders continue to have a vital leadership role in discernment and truth when nudged by the Holy Spirit to speak in meetings of worship and business. Sometimes individuals within the meeting tend to "outrun their Guide." One recorded minister referred to the ministry of elders as "speaking the truth of the Living Water of Christ Jesus." A labor of love. Those elders of a meeting with a gift of discernment are important. Sometimes the single prophetic voice speaks the discernment of God's will for the meeting. Just because someone speaks behind a seasoned elder or recorded minister to discredit what has been said by them, does not mean what has been spoken by an elder or recorded minister of the meeting should be ignored. The role of active elders and recorded ministers are an asset to the meeting's presiding clerk when discerning approval or disapproval of significant difficult decisions.

CHAPTER THIRTEEN

The Body of Christ, the Church
The Roman Women

We never know how unforeseen events in our lives will bring radical change. While Steve and I were pastoring at a Friends Church in Indiana one summer, I fell after stepping into a pot hole in our church parking lot during a Vacation Bible School event. This left me with a concussion, broken cheek bone, broken foot, and two broken arms at the same time! Having been basically healthy my entire life, it was a shock to become dependant upon others for daily necessities. Bones I had taken for granted were now unable to accomplish simple tasks: to get dressed in the morning, to prepare a meal and eat, and even to wipe a tear from my eye. I felt helpless.

It was during this time when I needed healing that I came to a new appreciation for the Body of Christ. The women of our church organized meals to be brought into our home each day for our family. They came with food to share with us and often stayed to talk and give encouragement. Many would pray with us. Notes and cards of encouragement were received. Ministry happened.

Most importantly, my two sisters took turns living with us and walked alongside our family during the physical therapy until I was able to drive. The Body of Christ, the church, was a blessing.

The New Testament Church, the Body of Christ

Paul wrote about the church being the Body of Christ in his epistle to the church of Rome. In the last chapter of Romans, we find examples of the Roman women and their variety of ministry roles in this New Testament church. This chapter is frequently unnoticed since the names of these women are veiled in Greek words with a feminine ending. This passage gives us an amazing example of how the Body of Christ embraced and appreciated women in ministry.

Phoebe is the first woman Paul introduces to us in Romans 16. With Phoebe we find Paul's description of church relationships termed in the language of a family. Paul describes Phoebe as "our sister." The Body of Jesus Christ, the church, is the family of God.

The second title given to Phoebe in Romans 16:1 by Paul is the Greek noun *diakonos*, at times translated as "deaconess." This word was used by Luke to describe Mary Magdalene and the ministering women. *Diakonos* described the emerging role of deacon in the New Testament church found in Luke 8:3. This Greek word was translated into English as "minister" by the early Tyndale Bible (1534) and the Geneva Bible (1560). According to *Young's Analytical Concordance to the Bible*, *diakonos* is translated deacon three times, servant seven times, and minister twenty times in the King James Bible (1611). When Paul refers to Phoebe as "a saint" we have a glimpse into her commitment to Jesus Christ. As "saints," God's divine *agape* love flows through them in ministry to others and their efforts are sanctified by the Holy Spirit. A saint reflects God's loving care with their life and ministry.

Finally, Paul refers to Phoebe as a patron or great helper, *prostatis*. As a female benefactor, she aided Paul's ministry and that of others from her personal finances (Romans 16:2). Noteworthy about Phoebe is that she is from the church of Cenchrea/Corinth, an early church plant by the ministry team of Paul, Priscilla, and Aquila, and the site of Apollos' subsequent ministry. The financial generosity of the New Testament women aided the spread of the gospel of Jesus Christ.

Priscilla, a known church planter with Paul, is greeted by him in this chapter. "Greet Priscilla and Aquila, my fellow workers in Christ Jesus. They risked their lives for me. Not only I but all the churches of the Gentiles are grateful to them" (Romans 16:3-4, NIV). In his epistle, Paul asks that his greeting be extended to the church in their home (Romans 16:5).

Junia is perhaps the biggest surprise (Romans 16:7). Paul described her as a leader in the Roman church and "prominent among the apostles." Andronicus seems to be her partner in ministry — perhaps her husband? Andronicus and Junia were described by Paul as "my relatives." Junia is credited as being in Christ before Paul. This astonishing leadership title is given to a woman who suffered as a prisoner for her faith. The story of her life is tucked away at the end of Romans 16!

Mary, Tryphena and **Tryphosa, Persis, Rufus' mother, Julia,** and **Nereus** are additional Roman women noted for their ministry. Mary is mentioned by Paul because she "has worked very hard among you" (Romans 16:6). Tryphena and Tryphosa are two women who are "workers in the Lord" (Romans 16:12). Persis is cited as having worked hard in the Lord, and is also called "beloved." A woman who was like a mother to Paul was the mother of Rufus (who was "chosen in the Lord"). Some believe Rufus is the son of Simon the Cyrenian, of Libya in northern Africa (Mark 15:21), who carried the cross of Jesus. Again, we find a familial title, that of mother, given to a noteworthy woman in the church. Paul concluded his epistle with greetings to the "saints who are with them," including two women — Julia and the sister of Nereus. As the New Testament Church developed, Paul clearly acknowledged the vital ministry leadership roles held by women who often traveled in ministry while preaching and teaching the gospel of the risen Christ, and at times suffered for their faith as did the first generation of Quaker women in the ministry.

Women in Ministry Among Friends

The vital role of twentieth century Friends women in the ministry is glimpsed within this sampling of Western Yearly Meeting Friends Church women ministers of Hamilton County, Indiana:

Fanny (Bates) Roberts Gentry

Born in Jolietville, Indiana, Fanny attended Union Bible College before entering the ministry. She served Friends at Eagle Creek, Hazel Dell, Mt. Lebanon, Phlox, Sycamore, and West Grove Friends. She was a frequent guest speaker among Friends. After the death of her first husband due to a traffic accident, she led a tent revival where her future husband came to the Lord. Her family remembered her practice to begin each day at the breakfast table with Scripture reading and prayer. When her grandson Steve was born, the family was told by the doctors that Steve would never walk. Fanny didn't believe it. She prayed! One day Steve's great aunt Myra held him by her finger urging toddler Steve to walk. When Myra felt a tap on her shoulders, she turned to see who was there and let go of Steve's fingers. Although she didn't see anyone, when she turned back to Steve, he miraculously took off running across the yard. Fanny believed in prayer.

Fanny Roberts Bates

Marilynn (Weaver) Bell

Marilynn's grandmother, Sibyl Rees Haworth, was a recorded Friends minister who served at Coloma Friends and lived with Marilynn's family. As a child Marilynn helped to take care of her grandmother who was blind, and was impressed at how much Scripture and how many hymns her grandmother had memorized. Marilynn attended Gray Friends as a child, and after her marriage attended Sheridan and Hortonville Friends. One day during meeting for worship, Marilynn's husband stated that he felt that his wife was a minister among Friends. The monthly meeting agreed! She was recorded in ministry by Western Yearly Meeting in 1982. Marilynn was called upon for visitation, to fill the pulpit, help at memorials, and serve as a representative for Western Yearly Meeting and Friends United Meeting ministries. She was a minister among the larger body of Friends.

Marilynn Bell

Mary Hiatt

Mary grew up at West Grove Friends and was a graduate of Cleveland Bible Institute. She was recorded in the ministry by

CHAPTER THIRTEEN: THE BODY OF CHRIST, THE CHURCH

Western Yearly Meeting in 1914. Mary was active in ministry among Friends at Courtland Avenue, Carmel, Sheridan, Second Friends, West Newton, Georgetown, Watseka, and Russiaville. She also served as an Assistant Superintendent of Western Yearly Meeting. Phyllis Rockhill (Carmel Friends) remembers being seriously ill at age five and asking her parents to have Mary Hiatt come to their home. Mary came to Phyllis' bedside to pray, sing, and hold the hand of this little girl. Phyllis recovered and became a cherished member among Hamilton County Friends.

Mary Hiatt

Frances Kinsey

When Frances was eight years old, she had a dream about the end of the world. When she woke up, she realized two very important things about this dream. The first was that the role of the church was to reach the lost, rather than to provide an escape for the members. The second thing was that she could not share this dream with the members of her church.* Frances pastored among Friends at Economy, Westland, Gray, and Hortonville.

Sarah Rayle

A graduate of Asbury, Sarah went into the ministry while she was in her forties, following the death of her husband. She was active in Friends pastoral ministry, quarterly meeting, and yearly meeting ministry activities. Sarah has been described by those who knew her as a "spitfire" preacher, strong in her beliefs and in stating them. She served in Friends pastoral ministry at Eagle Creek, Sheridan, Vermilion Grove, Newport, and Hinkle Creek. "She was a joy in ministry."

Sarah Rayle

---

*As told by Frances' daughter-in-law, Rosie.

Elizabeth Ann Murphy Reagan

Elizabeth was a recorded minister active in pastoral work for fifty years in Western Yearly Meeting at Lapel, Hortonville, Newberry, Lick Creek, Blue River, Paoli, West Union, and Coloma. At age fifty-six, she married recorded Friends minister Jehu Reagan. Elizabeth (1868–1958) is buried in Sheridan, Indiana. Elizabeth was "admired and loved by all," and shared she had a vision of the pearly gates as death approached.

Charlotte (Wilson) Scott

Charlotte felt led into ministry as a result of a miracle. One spring day her first-grade son, Charlie, was riding on the tractor with his dad. When his father jumped down from the tractor to shoot a groundhog in the field, he let his young son take the wheel. The front wheels of the tractor hit a field rock, and Charlie was thrown off and lodged underneath the tractor's disk. His father miraculously lifted the disk from his only son. He lived! Charlie was left with a scar on his back and his father with a scar on his face. After this incident, Charlotte and her husband said they were totally committed, and promised the Lord to place themselves into His hands, so that whatever the Lord put on their plates they would do.

As a recorded Friends woman minister, Charlotte served at Farr's Chapel in Tennessee, Westfield Friends, Dean of Women at William Penn College, Bolivia missionary work with Oregon Yearly Meeting, and eight years at Gray Friends. She was greatly influenced and encouraged by Sarah Rayle. Westfield Friends considered her a prayer warrior.

Sadie Vernon

A graduate of Earlham School of Religion, a Western Yearly Meeting recorded minister and a member of Carmel Friends Church, Sadie served as an FUM field staff member for several decades and was the "founding and guiding inspiration" for the Friends School in Belize City, Belize. Her concern was for Belize children with learning difficulties and she was the founder of the Christian Social Council.

Sadie Vernon

CHAPTER THIRTEEN: THE BODY OF CHRIST, THE CHURCH

What is impressive about these twentieth century Friends women ministers of Hamilton County, Indiana, was the appreciation people had of their spiritual maturity and ministry. The Holy Spirit led them to step out in faith in the midst of their unique circumstances to respond to ministry. Not only does the decline of recognizing, nurturing, and recording the spiritual gifts of women for public ministry show a decline of the spiritual vitality of Friends, but it negates one of the basic historic testimonies of the Religious Society of Friends. "There is neither Jew nor Gentile, neither slave nor free, nor is there male and female, for you are all one in Christ Jesus" (Galatians 3:28).

Letting Our Lives Speak in the Body of Christ

Too often our culture has been silent about the godly women in our country; their voices are often not heard. However, the "mothers" of the church are precious treasures that often serve as pillars of our families, churches, and communities. Their voices and the legacies of their lives are a pathway for those younger women who are just beginning their walk with the Lord. One of the younger attenders of the Chicago Fellowship of Friends once said that she wanted to come to the Friends women gatherings, because that is what she wanted to be like when she was that age. Their wisdom of faithfully walking with Jesus Christ is to be cherished.

We were in our late 20s when Steve and I were privileged to begin our mutual call to travel in the ministry among Friends. I realize now I was meeting the Friends women from what some have called the "greatest generation." Like the Apostle Paul, I have my own list of "spiritual mothers" who encouraged me and let the living water of Christ Jesus flow and minister to me!

Edna Smith (Iowa Yearly Meeting Elder)

Edna was the President of the United Society of Friends Women International, and advocated for our ministry at the Chicago Fellowship of Friends. I still remember sitting in her kitchen

Edna Smith

for a bowl of homemade potato soup after meeting for worship at Motor Friends. That day she also served up spiritual wisdom and encouragement for a young woman in Friends ministry. Edna was Mary Glenn Hadley's sister and Charlotte Stangeland's mother.

Charlotte Stangeland (Iowa Yearly Meeting Recorded Minister)

Charlotte is a prayer warrior who also has been a friend and spiritual consultant for ministry since our days at William Penn College and Penn Christian Fellowship. Besides serving on the faculty of William Penn University, pastoring and serving in numerous ways with Iowa Yearly Meeting, she launched the Friends Peace Curriculum for the Kenyan Friends Schools and helped with the early days of this book.

Charlotte Stangeland

Kara Newell Wilken (Indiana Yearly Meeting Recorded Minister)

Kara is a "seasoned Friend" who believed in the Chicago Fellowship of Friends ministry and opened the door for us to be on FUM's field staff. She eventually served as FUM General Secretary. Her hospitality and listening ears were a true gift to us in the early days of beginning the Chicago Fellowship of Friends ministry in Cabrini-Green. She encouraged me to pursue my theological education.

Kara Newell Wilken

Mary Ann White (Chicago Fellowship of Friends (WYM) Elder)

One of the first elders at the Chicago Fellowship of Friends, Mary Ann taught me to cook many Cabrini dishes. She was "mother" to so many of us! Mary Ann once said to an individual, "If you are not a Christian now, don't worry. Come to the Chicago Fellowship of Friends and you will be!"

Mary Ann White

CHAPTER THIRTEEN: THE BODY OF CHRIST, THE CHURCH

Joyce Hollingsworth
(Western Yearly Meeting Recorded Minister)

Joyce had a heart for the gospel of Jesus Christ and missions. She came from one of the earliest Friends meetings in Illinois, that sent Emory Reese to Kenya as a missionary from Western Yearly Meeting and FUM. When she spoke in meeting for business, I listened.

Joyce Hollingsworth

Mary Margaret Hubbard (Western Yearly Meeting, "Mother")

Mary Margaret gave me rides to USFW meetings, organized many Plainfield Friends Church and WYM meals, encouraged me to read from the church library, and modeled dedication to family and meeting — a true church mother who was a mother to many!

Mary Margaret Hubbard

Linda B. Selleck (Western Yearly Meeting Recorded Minister)

In our early days at the Chicago Fellowship of Friends, Linda and her husband Ron were in ministry at Chicago Monthly Meeting. Her work with FUM, Jamaica, Western, Indiana, and North Carolina Yearly Meetings has blessed many of us, as has her book, *Gentle Invaders: Quaker Women Educators and Racial Issues During the Civil War and Reconstruction*. Linda also researched and collected most of the artwork and photographs used in this book, including the book cover, and prepared them for publication. She located and contacted the organizations which held publishing rights for acknowledgement and copyright permission. Thank you for editing this book!

Linda B. Selleck

Audrey Sheets, Frances Haskett and Geneva Berry ("Mothers")

These women from our Westfield Friends USFW were active for the Lord among Friends even when in their nineties: Audrey Sheets, who listened, encouraged, cooked, and made homemade noodles for our mission fund-raising dinners even at the age of 96; Frances Haskett, who came to weekly Bible studies with her Bible even when her eyesight was failing (she had the glow of God's shekinah around her smiling face) and was also a monthly donor to the ministry at the Chicago Fellowship of Friends even before I knew her; and Geneva Berry (really a member of Hinkle Creek Friends who joined us at Westfield Friends USFW), who loved to whistle hymns even when she could no longer sing, baked persimmon pudding for our annual USFW fund raiser, and would give a testimony for the Lord working in her life! How precious to know these women.

Who are the spiritual women in your life that shared the "living water of Jesus Christ" with you? Who are the historic women your church has cherished? Can we invite today's "mothers and daughters" to form a supportive community for each other centered upon the simple joy found in Jesus Christ? Can we find ways to intentionally "irrigate" the lives of women in our community with the message of the gospel? Can we pray for a new generation of women to be empowered in leadership for outreach to our communities where many experience a spiritual drought?

Too often, faithful and holy women in the church have been passed over for leadership roles. Too often, young women in the church have been discouraged when they raise their voices to speak Truth to power — to protest narcissistic and abusive leadership in the church left unaddressed. Maybe there are holy women right now in your midst who are willing to discern, mentor, model, preach the full gospel of Christ Jesus, and teach spiritual leadership for the next generation.

Friends protested for religious freedom from a state church, for the freedom to preach the Truth of the gospel of Jesus Christ, and to worship and live according to our historic faith tenets and testimonies. They sacrificed for the rights of women during terrible persecutions, and for the right to preach from the leading of the Holy Spirit as recorded Ministers of the Gospel. Why should these freedoms be cancelled to accommodate the political pressure of syncretism?

CHAPTER THIRTEEN: THE BODY OF CHRIST, THE CHURCH

> *I pray that, according to the riches of His glory, He may grant that you may be strengthened in your inner being with power through His Spirit, and that Christ may dwell in your hearts through faith, as you are being rooted and grounded in love. I pray that you may have the power to comprehend, with all the saints, what is the breadth and length and height and depth, and to know the love of Christ that surpasses knowledge, so that you may be filled with all the fullness of God. Now to Him who by the power at work within us is able to accomplish abundantly far more than all we can ask or imagine, to Him be glory in the Church and in Christ Jesus to all generations, forever and ever. Amen.*
>
> — EPHESIANS 3:16-20
>
> *The God of peace be with all of you. Amen.*
>
> — ROMANS 15:33

This is an invitation to prayerful discernment to consider the lives of witnesses discussed in these scriptural passages, the historical evidence of recorded women in the ministry of the Friends Church (and the legacy of women in ministry in your own faith communities), and the personal testimonies of women who love the Lord. Your prayer life with the support of other women may transform your spiritual life or that of another. Your group may be the catalyst to revive a small country church or an urban store front church. You may be the encouragement a woman needs in ministry.

What follows is our Epilogue, then questions for individuals, spiritual friends, and study groups to journal or discuss alone or with others.

May we continue to lift up the living Christ Jesus, the head of the Body of Christ, the church, as we let our lives speak in ministry to the next generation.

It is time to be the change!

EPILOGUE

D. Elton Trueblood, born in Iowa, was a noted twentieth-century Quaker scholar and theologian. Author of thirty-three books, he once described America as a "cut flower civilization." At this moment in time, his words could easily describe much of the Christian church in America, including many groups of Friends.

In an attempt to be culturally and/or politically relevant, we have drifted into conflict over once-accepted faith tenets deeply anchored in scripture and have struggled with the pressure to align to popular norms and post-modern theology.

The central message of seventeenth-century Friends who were "restoring Primitive Christianity" as thousands of seekers joined their movement began wilting some time ago throughout the Society of Friends. Modern Friends too often struggled to communicate their faith, history, and formerly-held orthodox Christian beliefs to the next generation.

Many precious testimonies which had been grounded in a vibrant relationship with Jesus Christ as Savior and Friend, which recorded women had proclaimed throughout centuries of public ministry and writings, are now endangered.

Over the years, Linda has watched with sorrow as various national Friends programs, schools, and colleges removed references to Christian spiritual formation. Instead, these organizations and fellowships have shifted to identifying Friends groups for their social activism, and what are now referred to as Quaker core values. These are known as SPICES: simplicity, peace, integrity, community, equality, and stewardship. But these values are part of the cut flower process.

Orthodox Friends understand that these six values are a small part of the ever-expanding character of Christ, as revealed in scripture, and experienced during worship. When centered and gathered by the Holy Spirit, we experience the Living Christ as the Presence in our midst.

Recently Marlene attended a gathering for young adults who had grown up in the Friends Church. She listened with surprise as some of them wondered whether they had ever become official meeting members. With the church focused on new programs and outreach, we have often overlooked the need to nurture the interior spiritual life and growth of our young people.

Friends desire individuals to go to a deeper level of understanding of their faith, to walk in the inner sacraments of daily spiritual baptism and communion with Christ Jesus. By encountering the Living Christ in corporate worship and personal study and prayer, our Young Friends and newer adult members can discern the Holy Spirit's leading in their lives.

Younger and older people today continue to seek hope and long for an authentic friendship with Jesus Christ in a life-giving faith community that can be found with Friends.

Marlene remembers attending a Friends Summit Conference for young adults. There the need for such a book as *Simple Joy: Women, Ministry, Friends* was first revealed to her, and prompted her to begin writing this book. She said to herself — *"It is time!"*

MARLENE MORRISON PEDIGO, AUTHOR
LINDA B. SELLECK, EDITOR

> *... Christ [is] the Light of the world and lighteth every man [and woman] that cometh into the world ... You will say, Christ saith this, and the apostles say this; but what canst thou say? Art thou a child of Light and hast walked in the Light, and what thou speakest, is it inwardly from God?*
>
> — GEORGE FOX[1]

ENDNOTES

CHAPTER ONE *Listening Prayer and Obedience*

1. *The Journal of George Fox*, ed. Rufus M. Jones (Richmond, Indiana: Friends United Press, 1976), p. 66.
2. Ibid., p. 75.
3. Ibid., p. 82.
4. Ibid., pp. 88, 97.
5. Taylor, Ernest. E., *The Valiant Sixty* (London: The Bannisdale Press, 1951), pp. 40–41.
6. Punshon, John, *An Encounter with Silence: Reflections from the Quaker Tradition* (Richmond, Indiana: Friends United Press, 1987), pp. 36, 39.

CHAPTER TWO *Discernment*

1. Whiston, William, translator. *The Works of Josephus* (Peabody, Massachusetts, 1987), p. 370.
2. *A Sincere and Constant Love: An Introduction to the Work of Margaret Fell*, ed. T.H.S. Wallace, 2nd ed. (Richmond, Indiana: Friends United Press, 2009), p. 176.
3. Ibid., pp. 111, 118–119.

CHAPTER THREE *Evangelism*

1. *The Journal of George Fox*, ed. Rufus M. Jones, 186–187.
2. Bacon, Margaret Hope, *Mothers of Feminism: The Story of Quaker Women in America* (San Francisco, California: Harper & Row, 1986), p. 29.
3. *Wilt Thou Go On My Errand? Three 18th Century Journals of Quaker Women Ministers*, ed. Margaret Hope Bacon (Wallingford, Pennsylvania: Pendle Hill Publications, 1994), p. 47.
4. Ibid., p. 51.
5. *The Friends Library: Comprising Journals, Doctrinal Treatises, and Other Writings of Members of the Religious Society of Friends: Memoir of Ruth Follows*, ed. William Evans and Thomas Evans (Philadelphia, Pennsylvania: Joseph Rakestraw, 1840), p. 25.
6. Ibid., p. 26.
7. *A Sincere and Constant Love*, p. 15.

ENDNOTES

CHAPTER FOUR Peacemaker

1. *A Sincere and Constant Love*, pp. 89-90.
2. Plimpton, Ruth Talbot, *Mary Dyer, Biography of a Rebel Quaker* (Boston, Massachusetts: Branden Pub. Co., 1994), p. 188-189.
3. *The Minute Book of Western Yearly Meeting*, 1864, p. 19.
4. Selleck, Linda B., *Gentle Invaders: Quaker Women Educators and Racial Issues During the Civil War and Reconstruction* (Richmond, Indiana: Friends United Press, 1995), pp. 57-58.

CHAPTER FIVE Faith and Healing

1. *The Valiant Sixty*, p. 39.
2. *George Fox's 'Book of Miracles,'* ed. Henry J. Cadbury (Philadelphia, Pennsylvania: Friends General Conference, 2000), pp. 8-9.
3. *The Journal of Ann Branson, A Minister of the Gospel in the Society of Friends* (Philadelphia, Pennsylvania, c. 1892), p. 29-31.

CHAPTER SIX A Transformed Life Transforms Others

1. *The Memoir of the Life of Elizabeth Fry with Extracts From Her Journal and Letters*, ed. by her daughters Katharine Fry and Rachel Elizabeth Cresswell (Montclair, New Jersey: Patterson Smith, 1974), p. 36.
2. Lewis, Georgina King, *Elizabeth Fry* (London: Headley Brothers, c. 1909), pp. 27-28, 29.
3. *Memoir of the Life of Elizabeth Fry*, pp. 256, 258.
4. *Ibid.*, p. 262.
5. Lewis, *Elizabeth Fry*, pp. 52-53.
6. *Ibid.*, p. 53.
7. *The Life and Letters of Elizabeth L. Comstock*, ed. by her sister, Caroline Hare, (London: Headley Brothers, c. 1895), pp. 2-3.

CHAPTER SEVEN Deacon, Minister, Apostle

1. *Theological Dictionary of the New Testament, Vol. II*, ed. Gerhard Kittell (Grand Rapids, Michigan: Wm. B. Eerdmans Publishing Company, 1964), pp. 84, 85.
2. *Semi-Centennial Anniversary Western Yearly Meeting of Friends Church, 1858-1908* (Plainfield, Indiana: Publishing Association of Friends, 1908), pp. 159-160, 221-223.
3. *Ibid.*, pp. 149-150.
4. *Ibid.*, p. 150.
5. *Minutes of Western Yearly Meeting Friends Church*, Indiana, 1917, p. 115.

6. *Semi-Centennial Anniversary Western Yearly Meeting of Friends Church, 1858–1908*, p. 150.
7. *Minutes of Western Yearly Meeting of Friends, 1860*, p. 30.
8. *Semi-Centennial Anniversary Western Yearly Meeting of Friends Church, 1858–1908*, p. 152.
9. *Ibid.*, pp. 150–151.

CHAPTER EIGHT *Generosity*

1. Foster, Richard. *Celebration of Discipline: The Path to Spiritual Growth*, rev. ed. (San Francisco, California: Harper San Francisco, 1988), p. 33.
2. Cox, Eliza Armstrong, *Looking Back Over the Trail*, Women's Missionary Union of Friends in America (1927), p. 14.
3. Woolman, John. *The Journal of John Woolman and A Plea for the Poor* (Secaucus, New Jersey: The Citadel Press, 1961), pp. 11–12.
4. Wikipedia, s.v. "Explo '72," last modified June 30, 2022, https://en.wikipedia.org/wiki/Explo_'72.

CHAPTER NINE *Hospitality and Spirit Led Worship*

1. Oden, Thomas C., *The African Memory of Mark* (Downers Grove, Illinois: IVP Academic, 2011), p. 82.
2. Roberts, Arthur O. *Through Flaming Sword: The Life and Legacy of George Fox* (Newberg, Oregon: Barclay Press, 2008), p. 13.
3. *The Power of the Lord is Over All: The Pastoral Letters of George Fox*, ed. T. Canby Jones (Richmond, Indiana: Friends United Press, 1989), p. 176.
4. Kelly, Thomas R., *A Testament of Devotion* (New York, New York: Harper & Brothers, 1941), p. 54.
5. Trueblood, D. Elton, *The Incendiary Fellowship* (New York, New York: Harper & Row, 1967), pp. 107–108, 111.

CHAPTER ELEVEN *Lydia and the Women of Philippi*

1. Penn, William, *No Cross, No Crown*, ed. Ronald Selleck (Richmond, Indiana: Friends United Press, 1981), pp. vii–viii.
2. *Ibid.*, p. viii.
3. *The Journal of George Fox*, p. 77.
4. Bacon, Margaret Hope, *Mothers of Feminism*, p. 18.
5. "Mary Fisher," https://www.quakersintheworld.org/quakers-in-action/187
6. Sewel, William, *The History of the Rise, Increase, and Progress of the Christian People Called Quakers* (London: Forgotten Books, 2015), p. 294.

ENDNOTES

7. Van Dyke, Henry. *Poems of Henry Van Dyke*, 3rd ed., (New York: Charles Scribner's Sons, 1911), p. 332.

CHAPTER TWELVE *Church Planter and Elder*

1. Ford, Helen Kersey and Esther Ford Anderson, *The Steps of a Good Man Are Ordered by the Lord* (Pearl River, New York: African Inland Mission, 1951), p. 23.
2. *Ibid.*, p. 42.
3. *Ibid.*, p. 43.
4. *Ibid.*, pp. 83–84.

EPILOGUE

1. *A Sincere and Constant Love*, p. 176.

APPENDIX

Journal and Discuss with Faith Action

Chapter One

Journal and Discuss

Read Luke 1:26-38. How did Mary "let her life speak?"

Can you share a time when you knew God spoke to you? How did you respond?

Read Matthew 6:25-33. How does fear affect a call of God in our lives?

George Fox was a young man who was dissatisfied with what he saw spiritually happening in the church. He longed for something that would transform him. What actually brought about that transformation in Fox? What is required of us to experience Christ Jesus personally?

Queries for Discernment in the Church

Do you strive for the constant realization of God's presence in your life? Are you obedient to the leading and sensitive to the timing of the Holy Spirit? Do you use prayer, meditation, Bible study, and other devotional literature and disciplines to grow and mature spiritually? How do you seek to be a faithful steward of your life and all that God has entrusted to you? (*Faith and Practice of Indiana Yearly Meeting of the Religious Society of Friends*, 2011:40)

Prayer — Listening

How does being centered in Christ Jesus and walking daily in Christ's presence faciliate prayer? Why is listening prayer so important? Where is a quiet spot in your life that you can listen to God in prayer? How do you inwardly silence your heart so you can hear God's voice?

Faith in Action

Spend time in silent listening prayer as a group, known as "open worship" among programmed Friends. Close your meeting by sharing prayer concerns of the group, and then praying for the concerns expressed.

See if you can find time for listening prayer before your next meeting.

> *"Be still, and know that I am God!*
> *I am exalted among the nations,*
> *I am exalted in the earth."*
> *The Lord of hosts is with us;*
> *The God of Jacob is our refuge.*
>
> — PSALM 46:10–11

Chapter Two

Journal and Discuss

Read Luke 2:36–38. How did Anna "let her life speak?"

It was stated that "sanctuary seeped into Anna's soul." (pp. 7-8) How can sanctuary be internal as well as external? How have you experienced this?

Read Acts 15:6–20; 28. Consider the six elements of discernment in the New Testament church outlined from Acts 15. How effectively does your church incorporate each of these elements into decision-making? How might discernment be more effectively used in your meetings for business? What did Margaret Fell mean when she said, "We have taken scriptures in words, and know nothing of them in ourselves?" (p. 10) How are we sometimes guilty of this?

Queries for Discernment in the Church

Are meetings for worship and business held as scheduled and do you attend them consistently and on time? Do you come to meeting with heart and mind prepared for communion with God and fellowship with one another? Are your meetings for business conducted in a spirit of worship and a united search for God's leading in transacting the affairs of the meeting? Is the Meeting faithful in teaching and upholding Friends testimonies? (*Faith and Practice of Indiana Yearly Meeting of the Religious Society of Friends*, 2011:40-41)

Prayer — Discernment

Have you ever participated in a clearness committee or a meeting that modeled all the elements of prayer and discernment? Share about your experiences.

Faith in Action

If you are feeling a leading of the Holy Spirit for your future, you may want to consider forming a clearness committee to help you discern this leading. The following are suggestions for the process of forming a clearness committee.

> *I appeal to you therefore, brothers and sisters, by the mercies of God, To present your bodies as a living sacrifice, holy and acceptable to God, Which is your spiritual worship. Do not be conformed to this world, But be transformed by the renewing of your minds, So that you may discern what is the will of God — what is good and acceptable and perfect.*
>
> — ROMANS 12:1-2

Clearness Committee Discernment

Preparation:

1. The person seeking God's guidance and calling for a Clearness Committee may do so by prayerfully:
   a. inviting four or five spiritually mature people, who bring a variety of gifts to the group, to meet with her/him to seek direction or . . .
   b. asking the Ministry and Counsel (elders) to form such a group for clearness for him/her.
2. Arrange the place and time.
3. The person requesting a Clearness Committee should prepare a brief paragraph or two describing the issue she/he is facing, giving as many facts as are needed as background information. This can be done in writing and handed to the group to read when they are gathered, or it can be presented orally.

Instructions:

1. Choose a person who has a knowledge of clearness committees to clerk the meeting.
   a. The clerk opens the meeting, closes it, and keeps a sense of right order in between, making sure that the ground rules are followed, that everyone has the opportunity to speak.
   b. A recorder may be appointed if the person desires a record of questions asked and a summary of the responses.
2. Establish ground rules. For example:
   a. Determine the level of confidentiality this clearness committee is to have.
   b. Remember that questions are to be asked for the sake of the focus person's clarity, not the questioner's curiosity.
   c. This is not a time to present solutions or describe someone else's experience.
   d. The time together will be spent in a spirit of worship.

3. Outline the plan for the gathering.
   a. Open with silent waiting.
      i. When the focus person is ready, he/she will present a summary of the concern for which guidance is being sought.
   b. Members may then offer questions to bring clarification.
   c. Enter into a period of silent waiting.
   d. As the Holy Spirit leads, any person can speak out of the silence — give a message that may need to be shared, ask other questions, or . . .
   e. The clerk will ask the focus person how she/he wishes to proceed at this point.
   f. The focus person may
      i. Request more time of silence out of which anyone may speak following the same pattern as above.
      ii. Ask the committee to continue asking questions.
      iii. Draw together impressions he/she is gathering.
      iv. Ask the committee to give advice.
   g. Discuss if further plans need to be made for follow-up.
4. The spirit of this clearness committee should be undergirded with prayer, care, and love at the conclusion of the meeting. Members may feel a concern to continue to support the person in prayer and occasionally check in with the person to see how she/he is progressing.

(Taken from *Preparing Hearts and Minds*, by Anne Thomas and Mary Glenn Hadley, p. 21.)

Chapter Three

Journal and Discuss

Read John 4:1-42. How did the Samaritan woman "let her life speak" after meeting Jesus?

How does the living water of Christ Jesus flow in your life and your church, or is it more like a deep well?

APPENDIX: JOURNAL AND DISCUSS WITH FAITH ACTION

If someone were to ask you to explain baptism, how would you respond? If you overheard someone telling another person about Friends beliefs, and that person said that Friends don't believe in baptism, how could you correct that statement? When have you experienced a "deep baptism" in your life as you responded with obedience to the leadings of Christ Jesus?

Susanna Morris wrote in her Journal about being full of the "Reasoner." How easy is it for you to rationalize the status quo in your life, rather than come to the "Holy Baptizer" to be fit for service?

What does it mean to "earn the right to be heard" when you share about Christ Jesus with others? Talk about a time when you have attempted to share your faith with someone else. Were there "teachable ministry moments" for you? Were you willing to "pick up the cross" and move beyond the "dream stage" in sharing the gospel?

Queries for Discernment in the Church

Do you seek to live in constant communion with Jesus Christ? Do you partake of the Bread of Life and find refreshment in the Living Water, which is found in Jesus Christ alone? Do you experience baptism of the Holy Spirit, allowing every part of your life to come under the transforming influence of Christ's power, truth and love? Do you recognize that this life is found in a personal relationship with Jesus Christ and does not depend on any ritual, ceremony, or outward observance? Does your life bear testimony to this fact? *(Faith and Practice of Indiana Yearly Meeting of the Religious Society of Friends,* 2011:43)

Prayer — Intercession

Pray that you might be led to share your spiritual journey with another individual who is spiritually seeking.

Faith in Action

Simple evangelism is sharing our story with others who are spiritually thirsting. Take time to reflect upon your spiritual journey and create a spiritual timeline and/or collage (this may include

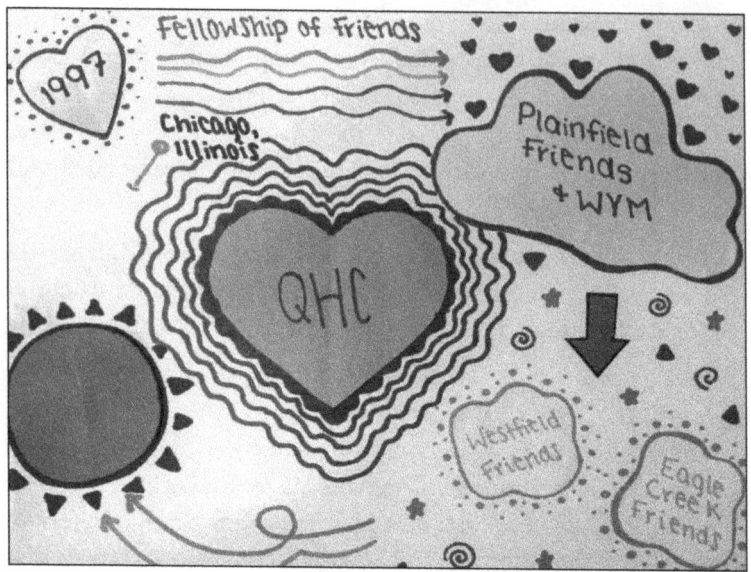

significant spiritual turning points where your faith was deepened, times of ministry from other Christians, joys and/or sorrows, and answered prayer). This tool of reflection can provide insight into how the Lord has been working in your life and become the basis of your personal testimony to share with others. This is a beautiful example of a spiritual timeline from my daughter.

Chapter Four

Journal and Discuss

Read Matthew 15:21-28. How did the Canaanite mother let her life speak?

Jesus was a good model of being a peacemaker in His interactions with people whose situations were pretty volatile, such as the time when he learned that John the Baptist had been beheaded. Handled differently, retaliation against the Roman authorities could have erupted leading to violence. What was it Jesus did instead that kept the situation peaceful? Why is prayer a first step of peacemaking? When we pray, do we really expect our prayers to be answered? How do you identify with the Canaanite mother?

Why is it important to confront the bondage of evil in our own lives? How does the power of the name of "Jesus" bring deliverance and peace? How do arrow and breath prayers bring peace into our daily lives?

How did Mary Dyer's death bring a unique witness to Truth and the importance of religious freedom to the American church? What is dangerous about a state church? What is your understanding of the Friends Peace Testimony?

Queries for Discernment in the Church

As Christians do you consistently practice principles of love and good will toward all God's people, toward the earth, and all creation? Do you work actively for peace and justice by living in such a way that harmony results? Do you endeavor to make clear to all whom you can influence, that war and the preparation for war is inconsistent with the spirit and teaching of Jesus Christ? How do you observe the testimony of Friends that leads toward creative, life-affirming ways of resolving conflict, and leads away from violence and destruction? (*Faith and Practice of Indiana Yearly Meeting of the Religious Society of Friends*, 2011:42)

Prayer — Arrow Prayers

Consider how the practice of arrow prayers would strengthen your spiritual growth. Reflect on daily events that occur in your life. What arrow prayers for thanksgiving to God have you noted? What does it mean to "pray without ceasing" in your life?

Faith in Action

When we first begin our Christian life, it is a good time to reflect on our relationships and pray about whether there are individuals to whom we need to make amends. It is easy to be in denial about our role in broken relationships. As you pray about your relationships, write down those individuals who come to mind where you may need to seek forgiveness. Pray further about sitting down to talk to them. Healing broken relationships is an important part of finding peace and living as a peacemaker.

Chapter Five

Journal and Discuss

Read Mark 5:21-43. How did the "Daughter" let her life speak?

Is the ministry of healing occurring in your church today? If yes, can you share how that ministry is being carried out? If no, can you discuss why you think Friends are not comfortable invoking prayers for healing? Do you believe God is capable of healing people today? Do you yearn for greater faith in God?

What stories can you share within your family where divine healing has taken place? Can you share a time in your life when you have experienced divine healing — physical, mental, and spiritual?

Queries for Discernment in the Church

Do you encourage your young people to choose a commitment to Jesus Christ and his church? Do you endeavor to instruct them in the principles and practices of Friends? Do you nurture the spiritual development of the youth of the meeting and promote their spiritual, mental and physical well-being? How do you involve and affirm the youth in the life of (your) meeting? (*Faith and Practice of Indiana Yearly Meeting of the Religious Society of Friends*, 2011:41)

Prayer — Prayer Lists

Praying with faith truly helps us become more intimate with God. What can you or your church do to help you develop in your faith? Does your church have a prayer list, prayer chain, or prayer meeting where you can unite your prayers for healing and intercession? Does your church invite people to center for open silent prayer together during meetings for worship?

Faith in Action

Sharing our message of faith with others is an amazing witness, particularly to those who are close to us and know us well. Sometimes writing down our testimony helps us to find the words to share it. Narrative journal writing as a part of daily devotions can become an important spiritual discipline in our life. Take time to share your legacy of faith with your small group.

The early Friends were famous for their narrative journals, which recorded how the Lord worked in their lives through calls to ministry, healings, powerful personal transformation, and stepping forward in ministry to address concerns. To understand the "school of the Holy Spirit" and how the Lord works, you may want to begin to collect the journals of the early Friends for your library. Why not start with George Fox and John Woolman? Enjoy!

> *Until now you have not asked for anything in my name. Ask and you will receive, so that your joy may be made complete.*
> — JOHN 16:24

Chapter Six

Journal and Discuss

Read Luke 7:36-50. How did the Anointing Woman let her life speak?

In what way does forgiveness empower personal restoration and generosity in ministry? How can spiritual pride exclude people from the church?

How do you live out your gratitude to Jesus or your passion for bringing about change in the lives of others? How are you motivated to serve others?

Is there someone(s) in your community with whom God is directing you to share Jesus' love? Is there a ministry this study group could do for your church or in your community or in collaboration with other Friends groups? Take time to discuss and pray together for God's leading.

Queries for Discernment in the Church

Are you concerned that our economic system shall so function as to sustain and enrich the life of all? Are you giving positive service to society in the promotion of peaceful methods of adjustment in all cases of social and industrial conflict? Do you support efforts which promote a humane criminal justice system and oppose the death penalty? Do you as workers, employers, producers, consumers and investors endeavor to cultivate good will and mutual understanding in your economic relationships? Do you intelligently exercise all of your constitutional privileges and thus seek to promote Christian influence locally, nationally, and internationally? (*Faith and Practice of Western Yearly Meeting of Friends Church*, 2005:29)

Prayer — Abiding Prayer

Why is abiding in Christ Jesus important in prayer? Spend part of your devotional time abiding in God's presence. When have you experienced Christ dwelling in you — what changed in you?

Faith in Action

What are the conditions of the criminal justice system in your area? Who is working for reform within the criminal justice system? Are "for-profit" prisons occurring in your state? Too often children in our communities die as a result of abuse and neglect. How many children are currently in foster care in your state/nation? How can you get involved with these concerns?

- Invite an advocate to come and speak about the condition of abused and neglected children in your region. What is being done in your area to protect individuals caught in domestic or sexual violence? Is there an organization you could support that helps victims of human trafficking trapped in the slave trade? Is there a shelter you could support?

- Plan a clothing drive or book drive for individuals who are being released from jail, or children and youth going into foster care. Donate Christmas gifts to children in foster care.

- Explore organizations which help women and men, youth and children escape human trafficking and discover how you can help. What is being done to help advocate for these people who continue to come up missing — particularly Native Americans?

- Explore how you can bless a foster family in your community. Provide an alternative to incarceration for teens. Get personally involved! It is time for clearness and reform!

Chapter Seven

Journal and Discuss

Read Luke 8:1–3. How did Mary Magdalene "let her life speak?"

What does it mean to experience deliverance from sin through Jesus Christ? Why is this important in the life of someone who feels called to ministry? How does your church embrace the *diakonos* ministry today? What is the history of women in the ministry in your church?

Read John 19:25b-27; 20:11-18. Where was Mary Magdalene during the crucifixion of Christ? What does it mean to have a ministry of presence in the midst of suffering? Why is this ministry important in the church today?

Mary Magdalene went from being a woman delivered from possession of demons, to becoming a recognized servant of Jesus Christ, to being commissioned to proclaim the message of Christ's resurrection to the disciples. Discuss how Mary Magdalene brings awareness for us of being called into ministry.

Queries for Discernment in the Church

Do you endeavor to recognize and develop your special talents and gifts for service in the Meeting and do you pray for divine guidance in their use? Do you cultivate the spiritual gifts of the members of your Meeting? Are you always ready to encourage and advise those who engage in the vocal ministry or in other Christian work? (*Faith and Practice of Indiana Yearly Meeting of the Religious Society of Friends*, 2011:44)

Prayer — Pocket Prayer Quilts and Faith in Action

Invite a recorded minister to share with you his/her call into ministry. How is a call to ministry discerned in your church?

Quilting has been a common activity of Friends women for generations. My mother passed on to me a pocket quilt (I believe from a woman in her neighborhood Sheridan United Methodist Church). This is a simple four patch quilt with a solid back. Inside is tucked away a cardboard cross which *can be felt to remind an individual to*

pray. God can take the broken pieces of our lives and make something beautiful. Maybe there is someone you know who would benefit from the gift of a pocket quilt you have made — a visual reminder you are praying for them. A prayer is pinned to the quilt:

> *This Pocket Prayer Quilt was made especially for you*
> *To slip into your pocket throughout the day.*
> *When your fingers touch the cross that is tucked*
> *Inside the quilt be mindful of God's love and grace for you.*
> *Keep it as a tangible symbol of the prayers that are*
> *Being said for you each day.*
> — AUTHOR UNKNOWN

Is there something you could do as a group to encourage prayer ministry in your church? Take time to discuss and pray together for God's leading.

APPENDIX: JOURNAL AND DISCUSS WITH FAITH ACTION

Chapter Eight

Journal and Discuss

Read Luke 10:38–42. How did Mary of Bethany "let her life speak?" Can you describe a time when listening to God in prayer brought you to the place of confessing your sin or need? In our busy lives, how well do we emphasize listening to God in our daily prayer life?

Read John 11:1–6. How did Mary of Bethany "let her life speak" in this passage? When we are brought through our darkest nights of despair, do we stop and give the Lord praise? Do the answers of prayer in our lives result in an apparent witness which is unmistakable by others? Is our abiding love for Christ Jesus and His restorative work in our lives reflected in agape service?

Read John 12:1–10. How did Mary of Bethany let "her life speak" in this passage? When someone does something for us, how well do we show our gratitude for what they do? Can you think of a time when someone let you know that something you did was important to them? How did it make you feel? Do we realize that expressing our gratitude to God brings Him joy?

Queries for Discernment in the Church

How do you individually accept responsibility for your rightful share of the worship, work and financial support of the Meeting and Friends broader shared concerns? (*Faith and Practice of Indiana Yearly Meeting of the Religious Society of Friends*, 2011:41)

Prayer — Gratitude Prayer Journal

Sometimes it is not easy to break old habits of complaining and self-centeredness. You may want to consider a daily gratitude prayer journal to help you focus upon the blessings of your life and to enhance your prayers of thanksgiving.

Faith in Action

As we grow in our relationship with Christ Jesus, we are motivated to service as an expression of the Lord's goodness in our lives. Discuss as a group organizing a "pitch-in" dinner for those who have provided important ministry in your life. Perhaps you would like to invite the pastor and his or her family for a "pitch-in" on a certain theme for a family fellowship night. You can provide a ministry to the families of your church by providing an inexpensive Friday night time of fellowship and family fun.

> Rejoice always, pray without ceasing, give thanks in all circumstances; For this is the will of God in Christ Jesus for you.
> — 1 THESSALONIANS 5:16-18

Chapter Nine

Journal and Discuss

Read Acts 12:1-19. How did Mary, the mother of Mark, "let her life speak?"

Why do you think gathering in a home for prayer enhances the prayer time together?

How would you define "gathered prayer" to someone who has heard the term but does not know what it means? Where have you experienced gathered prayer?

Read Matthew 18:20 and John 14:13-14. How does the Living Presence of Christ Jesus gather us for prayer in your church? Why is praying in the name of Jesus Christ important?

How significant is it that the early church seemed to emerge and grow away from the religious places of the day? Do we see that happening today? How can we experience more vital gathered prayer in our churches today?

Consider the Elton Trueblood quotation in chapter nine. Do you agree that the major power of the church never appears except in shared experience? Why or why not?

Queries for Discernment in the Church

Do you make your home a place of hospitality, friendliness, peace, and Christian fellowship? Do you consistently read the Bible? Do you read Christian devotional literature in your home, giving time for reverent meditation and prayer? Do you set a Christian example before your children and live in a way that promotes the sanctity and health of marriage and family life? Are you sensitive and do you minister to the needs of single people, single parent families; merged families and extended families? How do you provide instruction to your children for their spiritual lives; in educational, moral, and social issues of the day? (*Faith and Practice of Indiana Yearly Meeting of the Religious Society of Friends*, 2011:41)

Prayer — Gathered Prayer

The practice of a candlelight vigil on Christmas Eve is one of my favorite times of gathered prayer. To have individuals pass the light of a single candle throughout the meetinghouse until everyone's candle has been lit is a reminder that Christ is the Light of the world. Candlelight vigils today have become common when our communities have faced a public tragedy, personal crisis, or to mourn a loss. Perhaps a child has been abducted, a terrorist attack has occurred, or a horrible car accident has taken the lives of youth or adults in our community. Coming together for a candlelight vigil is a way to corporately mourn, to allow people to express their grief, and to seek that God would pour out His presence in our lives. In times of grief and tragedy spend time lifting up those in pain.

Faith in Action

Your group might want to gather for prayer. Lift up concerns you may have in your blessed community. Spend time in listening prayer and then corporately pray together. Before leaving, pass the Light of Christ to each other's individual candles. Pause in the silence to pray Paul's prayer for the church, found in Ephesians 3:20-21. Go in the peace of Christ Jesus!

Chapter Ten

Journal and Discuss

Read Acts 9:36-42. How did Tabitha/Dorcas "let her life speak?"

Many times the ministry of kind generosity happens without many people knowing about it until it comes out — maybe, like Dorcas, at the time of death. What should be your motivation in being generous with others? How would you define intercessory prayer? How do you see it as being a ministry of kindness and generosity? How can intercessory prayer become a greater part of the ministry of your group, your church?

Describe a time when through someone's kind generosity, you were especially blessed, encouraged, and given hope. Is your church — small group, Sunday School class, women's group — known for ministering generously in your community, yearly meeting, state, or world? In what way?

Queries for Discernment in the Church

Do you strive to educate yourselves and those in your care with the spiritual needs of the world? Do you support by prayer and systematic giving those who are laboring to extend the realm of Jesus Christ? Are you sensitive to the material needs of those within the meeting and in the local community? How do you use your spiritual gifts in serving humanity as God grants you light to see such service? (*Faith and Practice of Indiana Yearly Meeting of the Religious Society of Friends*, 2011:42)

Prayer — "Soaking" Prayer Partners

While in Cabrini-Green, one of our staff members would speak of the importance of prayer and the need to be "prayed up" when facing difficulties in life. As we began the Young Friends After-School program it was important to establish prayer support for the ministry: prayers for discernment, prayers that our ministry and its resources would increase, prayers for spiritual protection and covering, prayers that the message of the gospel would go forth into our community. Each circumstance of ministry will have its distinctive prayer needs. Soak in the presence of God and pray with others committed to the spiritual growth of your life and the church.

Faith in Action

In light of this lesson on the life of Tabitha/Dorcas and the signs of discipleship, what are the great needs of your community? How does your church demonstrate the mark of discipleship by "doing good and helping the poor?" What can you personally do to reach out in love beyond just financial giving? What can your group do?

> *Therefore, confess your sins to one another, and Pray for one another, so that you may be healed. The prayer of the righteous is powerful and effective.* — JAMES 5:16

Chapter Eleven

Journal and Discuss

Read Acts 16:11-40. How did the women of Philippi in this chapter "let their lives speak?"

Read Philippians 3:10. How do you respond to Paul's words when he says: "I want to know Christ . . . and the fellowship of His sufferings?" What does it mean to bear the "cross of Christ" today?

How have we benefited from the sufferings of people before us who have stood faithfully for their faith? Are Christians today suffering for our faith — here in this country or elsewhere? Can you share how you may have experienced some form of suffering for your faith?

How can we prepare ourselves to stand strong should persecution for our faith come to us? What role does praise and joy play in our lives when we suffer for our faith?

Queries for Discernment in the Church

Do you observe simplicity in your manner of living, so that devotion to Jesus Christ comes first in your life? Do you celebrate life as a gift of God? Do you recognize the extreme danger in the use of alcoholic beverages, tobacco and other destructive drugs? Do you refrain from their use? How do you actively avoid self-destructive stresses in your life? (*Faith and Practice of Indiana Yearly Meeting of the Religious Society of Friends*, 2011:41)

Prayer — Songs from the Heart

There is something about singing prayers of praise which lifts your spirit and can unite the church. Explore songs which are actually "sung scripture." Is there a testimony about the hymn writer which will further strengthen your faith? Consider the development of a play list of favorite Christian music which strengthens you.

Faith in Action

When I was a child we sometimes had a "singspiration" on a Sunday evening for families of our church. This was a casual night where people could call out the name of their favorite hymn and the pianist would play the hymn for the whole church to sing. Often the pastor would close the night with a message of praise and testimony.

> *Rejoice in the Lord always; again I will say, Rejoice. Let your gentleness be known to everyone. The Lord is near. Do not worry about anything, but in everything by prayer and supplication with thanksgiving let your requests be made known to God. And the peace of God, which surpasses all understanding, will guard your heart and your minds in Christ Jesus.*
> — PHILIPPIANS 4:4–7

Chapter Twelve

Journal and Discuss

Read Acts 18:24–28. How did Priscilla "let her life speak?"

How do we resolve cultural differences and work through conflict as our churches face a growing secular society? Are we destined to become large impersonal churches similar to the medieval cathedrals? Or perhaps, are we are becoming a politically correct church that forsakes the foundations of Christianity?

Read 1 Corinthians 16:19, 2 Timothy 4:19; Romans 16:3–5. How did Priscilla and Aquila's life take a detour? How did the Fords' life take a detour? How do you think God used the detours for good? Has your own life taken a detour from your stated goals? How did God use it for good?

Compare and contrast the culture of the Roman cities — Corinth, Ephesus, and Rome — with the culture of our cities today. How do we as individuals and churches move beyond our culture to communicate the gospel of Christ Jesus?

APPENDIX: JOURNAL AND DISCUSS WITH FAITH ACTION

Queries for Discernment in the Church

Does your attitude toward people of other races and gender indicate your belief in their right to equal opportunity? Do you believe in the spiritual capacity of all races and do you recognize their equality in the Sight of God? How do you fulfill your responsibility as a Christian to help in the elimination of racial, sexual, ethnic, religious and other forms of discrimination and prejudice? (*Faith and Practice of Indiana Yearly Meeting of the Religious Society of Friends*, 2011:42)

Prayers — Confession and Forgiveness

Sometimes our lives, families, or churches become spiritually "stuck." Consider gathering with those who are grounded in prayer ministry to pray for the historical "sin" or "wounds" in your life or that of the church. Take the concerns to the Lord in prayer and ask for spiritual healing and renewal. Call upon the ministry of elders and recorded ministers.

Faith in Action

The Kenyan Friends Church is growing and always has projects which need financial support. Has anyone in your area been to Kenya, and are they able to share about what is currently happening? Can you research what projects are in need of support? Explore the possibility of sharing your research. Give your church a challenge to take up a special offering or organize a fund-raising event to help the Kenyan Friends Church continue to plant new churches!

> *For where two or three are gathered in my name, I am there among them.* — MATTHEW 18:20

Chapter Thirteen

Journal and Discuss

Read Romans 16. How did the women mentioned by Paul in Romans 16 "let their lives speak?"

Why do you think the early church used the language of the family to describe the relationships they had with each other? What indicators do you find in this text that leadership in the church reflected an individual's spiritual maturity and deep commitment?

What roles of ministry occur among the women of your church? How does your church encourage women in ministry? Who are the women in ministry that have made an impact in your life? Are there common traits among these women? How do they "let their lives speak?"

How does your church discern the nomination of members to use their spiritual gifts within the Body of Christ? In what ways does your church offer appreciation for those who minister within the Body of Christ? How can we find greater opportunities to celebrate the spiritual gifts within the Body of Christ? How does the Body of Christ Jesus let their lives speak today?

Queries for Discernment in the Church

How is God's presence regularly experienced in the shared life of your Meeting? What does your Meeting do to help individual Friends to experience the sacredness of Christ's presence in their homes, family relationships, work places, leisure activities, and relationships with neighbors? What does the consistent remembrance and awareness of Jesus' sacrificial forgiveness motivate your Meeting to do, to express the same loving grace to one another and to people beyond the Church? What does your Meeting do sacrificially for others with nothing expected in return? In what ways is the life of your Meeting community nourishing and nurturing new spiritual maturity and growth? (*Faith and Practice of Indiana Yearly Meeting of the Religious Society of Friends*, 2011:43)

Prayer — Walks

While in Cabrini-Green, the churches would gather on Good Friday for a prayer walk in our community. We would carry a cross with us and stop at certain "hot spots" in our community to read scriptures and pray. People from the neighborhood would join us on the prayer walks. These heightened spiral experiences drew us closer to the Lord and to each other.

APPENDIX: JOURNAL AND DISCUSS WITH FAITH ACTION

Another prayer practice I have had is to have a prayer walk in the meetinghouse where I worship. I walk around the meetingroom, and and then stop and pray for individuals and for families where they usually sit during worship. All the leaders in our churches and communities need to be covered by prayer.

Faith in Action

Consider organizing a pitch-in or carry-in meal with those in your small group. If time permits, you may want to watch the movie *Friendly Persuasion*, which is the story of a Friends woman minister and her life during the time of the Civil War. Perhaps you would like to share a passage or two from your journal writings. How have you let your life speak? What do you believe is your own spiritual legacy?

Acknowledgements for Photographs and Art Work

COVER

Quaker Woman Preaching to Dutch Settlers in the Streets of New Amsterdam, 1657. Anonymous wood carving. Woodcut from Alamy Stock Images.

CHAPTER ONE

The Annunciation. Artwork by Henry Ossawa Tanner (1859–1937), black and white image used with permission by the Philadelphia Museum of Art, purchased with the W.P. Wilstach Fund, 1899.

Quaker Woman Preaching to Dutch Settlers in the Streets of New Amsterdam, 1657 (now New York City). Anonymous wood carving. Alamy Stock Images.

William Green Homes, Chicago's Cabrini-Green Public Housing. Library of Congress.

CHAPTER TWO

George Fox at Swarthmore Hall with the Fell Family. Etching by Robert Spence (1871–1964). Used by permission of the Quaker and Special Collections, Haverford College, Haverford, Pennsylvania.

Swarthmore Hall. Artwork by George Lehman (1800–1870). From the Pennsylvania Academy for the Fine Arts, John S. Phillips Collection.

CHAPTER THREE

George Fox, Leopold Grozelier (1830–1865). Alamy Stock Images.

1723 Quaker Meeting in London — A Female Quaker Preaches from the Balcony. By Bernard Picard (1673–1733), engraving by Pieter Tanje (1706–1761). Alamy Stock Images.

ACKNOWLEDGEMENTS FOR PHOTOGRAPHS AND ART WORK

CHAPTER FOUR

Statue of Mary Dyer, Sylvia Shaw Judson. Located in front of the Stout Meetinghouse on the Earlham College campus, Richmond, Indiana. Used by permission of the Earlham Photograph Collection and College Archives.

On the Way to School — Students going to the Penn School on the Sea Islands of South Carolina. From *Letters and Diary of Laura M. Towne: Written from the Sea Islands of South Carolina.* (Cambridge: Riverside Press, 1912), 200.

CHAPTER FIVE

The Message, by J. Walter West (1860-1933). Used by permission of Britain Yearly Meeting.

Steve and Marlene Pedigo on Oak Street in Cabrini-Green: Chicago Fellowship of Friends Co-Pastors. Personal collection of Marlene Pedigo.

The Chicago Fellowship of Friends, 515 West Oak, Chicago, Illinois. Personal collection of Marlene Pedigo.

CHAPTER SIX

Elizabeth Fry, anonymous, used by permission of Friends Historical Library of Swartmore College.

Mrs. Fry Reading to the Prisoners in Newgate in the Year 1816. 1863 photograph by Thomas Oldham Barlow (1823-1889) of the original painting by Jerry Barrett (1823-1906). Used by permission of Britain Yearly Meeting.

Elizabeth L. Comstock (1815-1891). Photographer unknown. From *Life and Letters of Elizabeth L. Comstock*, c. 1895.

The Chicago Fellowship of Friends, by Lucy Sikes. Personal collection of Marlene Pedigo.

CHAPTER SEVEN

Drusilla Wilson, 1858. Photograph used by permission of Western Yearly Meeting, from *Western Yearly Meeting Semi-Centennial Anniversary Book.*

CHAPTER EIGHT

Silent Meeting, by J. Walter West (1860-1933). Used by permission of Britain Yearly Meeting.

Eliza Armstrong Cox (1850-1935). Photograph used by permission of Western Yearly Meeting, from *Western Yearly Meeting of Friends Church Semi-Centennial Anniversary Book.*

Mary Glenn Hadley with Student Nurses in Kenya. Photograph used by permission of Charlotte Stangeland, from her personal collection.

CHAPTER NINE

The Grace Church Street Meeting House. Artist unknown. Used by permission of the Quaker and Special Collections, Haverford College, Haverford, Pennsylvania.

The Presence in the Midst, by James Doyle Penrose (1862–1932). Used by permission of Britain Yearly Meeting.

Charlotte Thomas and Student Condra Working at the Young Friends After-School Program at the Chicago Fellowship of Friends. Personal collection of Marlene Pedigo.

CHAPTER TEN

Kenyan Women's Gathering at the United Society of Friends Women in Kenya. Used by permission of Friends United Meeting.

CHAPTER ELEVEN

Cabrini High Rise Apartments, 1159-61 N. Larrabee, Chicago, Illinois. Personal collection of Marlene Pedigo.

Mary Fisher Before the Sultan of the Ottoman Empire. Artist unknown. Alamy Stock Images.

CHAPTER TWELVE

Helen and Jefferson Ford with Family, 1911. Photographer unknown. From *The Steps of a Good Man.* Used by permission of Friends United Meeting.

Grinnell Friends Church, Grinnell, Iowa. Personal collection of Marlene Pedigo.

CHAPTER THIRTEEN

Fanny (Bates) Roberts Gentry. Used by permission of Steve Roberts.

Marilynn (Weaver) Bell. Used with her permission.

Mary Hiatt. Used by permission of Kelly Haemmerle from the Hinkle Creek Friends collection.

Sarah Rayle. Used by permission of Kelly Haemmerle from the Hinkle Creek Friends collection.

Elizabeth Ann Murphy Reagan. Used by permission of Pam Sims.

Sadie Vernon. Used by permission of Earlham College.

ACKNOWLEDGEMENTS FOR PHOTOGRAPHS AND ART WORK

Edna Smith. Used by permission of Charlotte Stangeland.

Charlotte Stangeland. Used by her permission.

Kara Newell Wilkens. Used by her permission.

Mary Ann White. Personal collection of Marlene Pedigo.

Joyce Hollingsworth. Used by permission of Pastor Jim Hollingsworth.

Mary Margaret Hubbard. Used by permission of Brenda Hubbard Jackson.

Linda B. Selleck. Used by her permission.

APPENDIX

Faith in Action Timeline Collage. Personal collection of Marlene Pedigo.

Pocket Prayer Quilts. Personal collection of Marlene Pedigo.

BIBLIOGRAPHY

Arnold, Clinton E., general ed. *Zondervan Illustrated Bible Backgrounds Commentary*, Vol. 1. Grand Rapids, MI: Zondervan, 2002.

Bacon, Margaret Hope. *Mothers of Feminism, The Story of Quaker Women in America*. San Francisco: Harper & Row, 1986.

_____, ed. *Wilt Thou Go on My Errand? Journals of Three 18th Century Quaker Women Ministers: Susanna Morris 1682–1755, Elizabeth Hudson 1722–1783, Ann Moore 1710–1783*. Wallingford, PA: Pendle Hill Publications, 1994.

Barclay, Robert. *Anarchy of the Ranters*. Philadelphia, PA: Solomon W. Conrad, 1822.

Barter, Byron; Neal, Stuart; Roberts, Leanna; Roberts, Joseph. *A History of Westfield and Washington Township*. Noblesville, IN: Image Builders, 1997.

Besse, Joseph. *A Collection of the Sufferings of the People called Quakers*, Vol. 2. London: British Library Reproduction, 1753.

Cadbury, Henry J., ed. *George Fox's Book of Miracles*. Richmond, IN: Friends United Press, 2000.

Card, Michael. *Luke, The Gospel of Amazement*. Downers Grove, IL: IVP Books, 2011.

Common Bible, New Revised Standard Version. Nashville: Thomas Nelson Publishers, 1989.

Cox, Eliza Armstrong. *Looking Back Over the Trail*. Women's Missionary Union of Friends in America, 1927.

Evans, William and Thomas, ed. *Friends Library*, Vol. IV. Philadelphia, PA: Joseph Rakestraw, 1840.

Faith and Practice of Indiana Yearly Meeting of the Religious Society of Friends. Muncie, IN: Indiana Yearly Meeting, 2011.

Faith and Practice of Western Yearly Meeting of Friends Church, 2005. Plainfield, IN: Starkin Printing, 2005.

Ford, Helen Kersey and Esther Ford Anderson. *The Steps of a Good Man*. Pearl River, NY: Africa Inland Mission, 1951.

Foster, Richard. *Celebration of Discipline*. San Francisco: Harper, 1988.

_____. *Streams of Living Water*. San Francisco: Harper, 1998.

Fry, Katharine and Rachel Elizabeth Cresswell, ed. *Memoir of the Life Elizabeth Fry with Extracts From Her Journal and Letters*. Montclair, NJ: Patterson Smith, 1974.

Hare, Caroline, ed. *Life and Letters of Elizabeth L. Comstock*. Philadelphia, PA: J.C. Winston & Co., 1895.

Jones, Rufus M., ed. *The Journal of George Fox*. Richmond, IN: Friends United Press, 1976.

Jones, T. Canby, ed. *The Power of the Lord is Over All: The Pastoral Letters of George Fox*. Richmond, IN: Friends United Press, 1989.

Josephus. *The Works of Josephus*. William Whiston, trans. Peabody, MA:Hendrikson Publishers, 1987.

Kelly, Thomas R. *A Testament of Devotion*. New York: Harper & Brothers, 1992.

Kittel, Gerhard, ed. *Theological Dictionary of the New Testament*, Vol. I and II, Grand Rapids, MI: Wm. B. Eerdmans Pub., 2006.

Lewis, Georgina King. *Elizabeth Fry*. London: Headley Brothers, 1909.

Locker, Clara Lee Hadley and Stangeland, Charlotte, ed. *Led by the Light*, 2021.

Lumb, Judy, ed. *In-Transit: The Story of a Journey*. Belize City, Belize: The Angelus Press, 2000.

Martin, Marcelle. *Mary Fisher: Maidservant Turned Prophet*. Philadelphia: *Friends Journal*, 2.1.2008.

McDonald, Hope. *Discovering How to Pray*. Grand Rapids, MI: Zondervan, 1976.

Oden, Thomas C. *The African Memory of Mark, Reassessing Early Church Tradition*. Downers Grove, IL: IVP Academic, 2011.

Penn, William. *No Cross, No Crown*. Ronald Selleck, ed. Richmond, IN: Friends United Press, 1981.

Plimpton, Ruth Talbot. *Mary Dyer, Biography of a Rebel Quaker*. Boston, MA: Branden Pub. Co., 1994.

Punshon, John. *Encounter with Silence: Reflections from the Quaker Tradition*. Richmond, IN: Friends United Press, 1987.

Roberts, Arthur O. *Through the Flaming Sword:The Life and legacy of George Fox*. Newburg, OR: Barclay Press, 2008.

Roberts, Leanna; Neal Stuart; Byron Barker; Joseph Roberts. *Our Westfield: A History of Westfield and Washington Township*. Noblesville, IN: Rowland Printing, 1997.

Selleck, Linda B. *Gentle Invaders: Quaker Women Educators and Racial Issues During the Civil War and Reconstruction*. Richmond, IN: Friends United Press, 1995.

Semi-Centennial Anniversary of Western Yearly Meeting of Friends Church. Plainfield, IN: Publishing Association of Friends, 1908.

Sewel, William. *History of the Rise, Increase, and Progress of the Christian People Called Quakers*, Vol. I and Vol. II, Philadelphia: Friends Bookstore, 1856.

Taylor, Ernest E. *The Valiant Sixty*. London: The Bannisdale Press, 1951.

Thomas, Anne and Mary Glenn Hadley, eds. *Preparing Hearts and Minds*. Richmond, IN: Friends United Press

Trevett, Christine. *Women and Quakerism in the 17th Century*. York, England: The Ebor Press, 1991.

Trueblood, D. Elton. *The Incendiary Fellowship*. New York: Harper & Row, 1967.

_____. *The People Called Quakers*. New York: Harper & Row, 1966.

Van Dyke, Henry. *Poems of Henry Van Dyke*. 3rd ed., New York: Charles Scribner's Sons, 1911.

Vipoint, Elfrida. *George Fox and the Valiant Sixty*. Philadelphia, PA: Friends General Conference, 1975.

Wallace, T.H.S., ed. *A Sincere and Constant Love: An Introduction to the Work of Margaret Fell*. Richmond, IN: Friends United Press, 1992.

Western Yearly Meeting of Friends Church Minute Book. Noblesville, IN: Butler Printing, 1917.

Whiston, William, Translator. *The Works of Josephus*. Peabody, MA: Hendrikson Publishers, 1987.

Woolman, John. *The Journal of John Woolman and A Plea for the Poor*. Secaucus, NJ: The Citadel Press, 1961.

Young, Robert. *The Analytical Concordance to the Bible*. Grand Rapids, MI: Wm. B. Eerdmans Publishing Company, 1970.

www.ingramcontent.com/pod-product-compliance
Lightning Source LLC
LaVergne TN
LVHW041623070426
835507LV00008B/424